THE WHITE HOUSE
CHANDELIERS

AN AUTOBIOGRAPHY OF
STEWART CALVIN AND JANICE M. STEVENS

THE WHITE HOUSE CHANDELIERS

HISTORY BEHIND THE WALLS
OF 7 U.S. PRESIDENTS

LYNETTA G. STEVENS

CITI OF
BOOKS

CITIOFBOOKS, INC.
3736 Eubank NE Suite A1
Albuquerque, NM 87111-3579
www.citiofbooks.com
Hotline: 1 (877) 389-2759
Fax: 1 (505) 930-7244

Ordering Information:

Quantity sales. Special discounts are available on quantity purchases by corporations, associations, and others. For details, contact the publisher at the address above.

Printed in the United States of America.

ISBN-13:   Softcover   978-1-962366-89-2
                Ebook   978-1-962366-90-8
                Hardcover   978-1-962366-91-5

Library of Congress Control Number: 2023921306

CONTENTS

Acknowledgements 7

Introduction 11

Preface 13

Dedication 15

EARLY BEGINNINGS

My Childhood 17

Endeavors 27

All Things Considered 35

Fort Knox, Kentucky To Augusta, Georgia And Back 39

Germany 47

Post Germany 53

WHITE HOUSE HERE I COME

Stewart "Calvin" And Janice "Marie" 62

How I Got There 65

Family Life While Working At The White House 74

My Faith 90

THE CHANDELIER HISTORY FACTS and LIFE

A Glimpse From The Top: The History Of The Chandeliers 98

Chandelier Elegance 102

All-Around Good Guy 112

The Journey: A Work In Progress 122

FORWORD ON THE U.S. PRESIDENTS

President Richard M. Nixon 133

President Gerald R. Ford 137

President James E. Carter, Jr. 140

President Ronald W. Regan 146

President George H.W. Bush 153

President William J. Clinton 156

President George W. Bush 162

In Honorarium Of The 44th President, Barack H. Obama................................168

Tribute To The First Ladies.. 170

Advice To The Young Generation... 172

Historical Notes 176

Behind The Scenes Gallery Of The Whitehouse Portraits................................ 179

Stewart Calvin Stevens Sr.. 181

Presidential Remarks About Stewart C. Stevens Sr... 185

ACKNOWLEDGEMENTS

Stewart C. Stevens, Sr. starts his story sharing how he felt over the course of his life/.

This is a Tribute to you, Mom and Dad, and in knowing you did the best that you could possibly do, helps me to understand the why.

While life takes us to our next destination, it's with great assurance that you both, Mom and Dad, would be pleased. Through embarking upon this journey of keeping your story alive and in continuance of your Legacy...much gratitude for the years we all had together. Your lives in pictures with history of your White House story is my autobiography tribute.

And I Quote: William Wordsworth (courtesy of the poet William Wordsworth)

"What though the radiance which was once so bright
Be now forever taken from my sight,
Though nothing can bring back the hour
Of Splendor in the grass, of glory in the flower?
I will grieve not, rather find
Strength in what remains behind
In the primal sympathy
Which, having been, must ever be.
In the soothing thoughts that spring
Out of human suffering,
In the faith that looks through death,
In years that bring the philosophic mind."

With much gratitude ….Gone But Never Forgotten, With Love

OVER THE COURSE OF my entire life, I figure I have been passed over, misunderstood, and at times overworked and placed in a position to carry the "weight of the world" on my shoulders, literally, in order to maintain the best life possible for myself, for the family I was born into, and for my immediate family, which was no burden to me at all because I cared and loved deeply for my family.

I know I have touched so many lives and my life has been an example to others. However, at last I am here writing a book about my life and my life story. If my life has not already done so, hopefully this book will touch many others in a very special way.

First and foremost, I want to thank my Heavenly Father for all that I have encountered and endured throughout my life. Otherwise, none of it would have been possible. While I was just a small child, I was in training for the work I was to do. It was because of Him that I landed at the White House as The Chandelier Polisher and Window Washer.

Last, but not least, if it had not been for my darling first and last love, my wife Janice "Marie" Stevens, who had the love, patience and endurance to support me even when things looked so bleak before coming on board at the White House, I am not sure how I would have fared. She has been the wind beneath my wing and is now the "Angel" above my head. She helped me and continued through the course of my life. I want to thank Marie, for giving me wonderful children and through them grandchildren and great grandchildren.

A lot of thanks and gratitude goes out to the White House Staff, and Chief Usher Mr. Rex Scouten, Assistant Chief Usher Mr. Gary Walters, Housekeeping Supervisor Mrs. Christine Crans- Limerick. And, thanks to the White House Historical Association and all of the people who have supported me over the years.

To those who read this book, thank you for your support. You'll have a lot of good stories, but also beautiful pictures of the White House and my family. Through this book, I've opened up the world of the White House with stories, art, and photography. I know you will enjoy it!

INTRODUCTION

In many ways, we may feel that we need an introduction and of course that depends on whether you have had a name given to you such as Stewart Calvin Stevens. ` It was of great benefit that Stewart wanted to introduce himself to everyone! On the personal part of Stewart's history not just history of The Chandeliers, let's elaborate on a few points. There are many people in the world that have acquired uniqueness, and he was one of them. The Chandeliers were not unique, he was! He was because …. Just because. The polishing was what he did as a career; we are not just speaking of a career; but, the man, the person, the individual and what he exemplified.

Stewart exemplified, living through hard times during adversity, being in touch with your inner spiritual being (not religion; spirituality) enough to know when it's time to go to the next level, operating in faith and confidence (It took a lot of faith one would think to get up there each day and the confidence that you could do it all perfectly without breaking anything), and even prior to the White House, Stewart Calvin had faith that if he got out of the Marshall Heights community, he would excel. If not graduating from grade school, he would most assuredly graduate from the Military Academy. He set goals for himself.

IF YOU ASK ANYONE whether they've heard of Stewart C. Stevens, Senior, the White House Chandelier Polisher, they probably would say, "Who is he?" For the most part, I am not very popular or sought after because I have been a rather behind-the-scenes type of guy and have strictly operated that way even in my job. What is amazing is how on most occasions when photographers or cameramen arrived, they liked to photograph me. I am photogenic and didn't mind this while performing my job at the White House. They didn't mind either; so much so that my signature pose was featured frequently in the book,

"The Working White House" had me on display. Being on display was not something I encouraged because I believe your works will speak for you without tooting your own horn. All in all though, I am thankful for the opportunity to have been placed in a position some people would wonder about – how a Black man in the 70's got to work in "high" places such as I. Some even asked, "How did you get here and who did you know." It was obviously rather bizarre to me also. I did not have a lot of education, but I had confidence in myself that I could do whatever I set out to do and that it all came from reaching down inside of my inner man and saying "You've got this. You can do this, Steve," even when no one encouraged me. I had the belief it could be done and that I could do better for myself. My circumstances did not rule who I am or who I was, but what's very important is where I was going. In my DNA were ingredients such as integrity, survivorship, and stewardship. My mother even named me the appropriate name, "Stewart," which is defined as keeper of the house; one who is in charge of a large estate; an official who supervises or assists in the management of an event. This is my legacy.

PREFACE

Stewart felt it necessary to explain the variety of names he was given. People would say to him, "You have 2 last names". "Yes", he would reply. "Is Stewart your last name or is it Stevens?" People would ask. "Well who is Calvin?" Coming to this conclusion, that you can be one person, yet it depends on to whom you are in relation to the individual.

While growing up at home, he was Calvin. To his wife, he's Calvin (middle names were used as a custom in that era). To the schools and military, he's Stewart. To the White House, he's Steve (short for Stevens). To me, he's Daddy and Dad.

GOOD MORNING LADIES AND gentlemen, young men and young women, my name is Stewart Calvin Stevens, Senior. I would like to tell you a story about my life. I have had several names in my lifetime. In my early life at home, everyone called me *Calvin*. In my early life at school, teachers and classmates called me *Stewart*. The Presidents and White House staff addressed me as *Steve*. I am introducing myself to the world as Stewart Calvin Stevens, SR., otherwise known as the White House *Chandelier Polisher Specialist*. Regarding my job while working at the White House, my initial title was Custodial Specialist. My job was to clean all the chandeliers, windows (inside and out), candelabras, wall sconces, and light globes. The supervisor who created the title of Chandelier Polishing Specialist was Mrs. Christine Crans-Limerick. She created the title based on how well I performed my job. To my knowledge, I am the only one who ever worked under this title at the White House. I cannot be for certain, but I believe it to be. However, this title was assigned to me because of what I did and how well I did it.

DEDICATION

This newly-branded and published book, The White House Chandeliers, History Behind the Walls of Seven U.S. Presidents is my dedication to you both Mother and Father. May you both Rest in Peace with the Angels. May you receive your Rewards for all your hard Labor and the Love you tried to give in this Life. You both gave to help so many and elaboration is mainly on your spoken words. It is With Love,

THIS BOOK IS DEDICATED to my first and only love, Janice Marie Stevens. Darling, without you I would not have been able to do the job at the White House. As my First Lady, this book is written in memory of you.

All my Love, Stewart "Calvin" Stevens

PART I:
EARLY BEGINNINGS

MY CHILDHOOD

Calvin's childhood was not easy and that is what has been spoken while telling his story; I state as he simply explained.

Stewart "Calvin" (Better known as Calvin in childhood so for this sake; let's refer to him as "Calvin") Calvin told me of an aunt that worked him tremendously. She would get him up there and have him to pick oranges or some kind of fruit from her trees. She'd then say, "You look so much like your daddy" and this was impressive to him (who wouldn't want to look like their father or mother?) Well, when it came time to pay up, she would drop him a quarter or claim she did not have any money. Calvin shared that he and some brothers worked to clean up a cemetery in Washington, DC and make a little change. There's not a doubt in anyone's mind that Calvin would work and did not like to be ridiculed.

He was never looking for anyone to give him anything. What he did not like was being taken advantage of..., who does? I guess, I surely have these genes!

At times he would hang in the alleys behind the house he grew up in; hanging out with an old buddy way back when, times were tough

He played cards and as teenage years rolled by he would hang out with Marie's eldest brother playing Horseshoes. They were very close...Calvin and the brother of Marie.

There was no sewer water in the homes back then; so outside toilets were the bathrooms; (we call them Porta Johns today). At times, when it was really cold, the children would hold themselves which later in life could do a number on the digestive system, unfortunately. Water was carried in from the outside pumps for bathing and dish washing.

Since money was scarce in those days. There was little or no entertainment except card playing, checkers, dice shooting, house parties and plenty of love-making! Stewart grew up in the "Silent Generation". People of this generation and especially blacks kept silent so as to not make waves and work was not easy to find.

This generation was a product of the Great Depression --you only had a few pair of shoes if that and food was scarce. It was not easy being born in such a large family and definitely not so with so many mouths to feed. Throughout these tumultuous times, edible staples consisted of beans, rice, and potatoes which fortified the body. Yet, food insecurity and other familial conditions can make for chaos. Empty stomachs make for less concentration in school—unfortunately, that's what he endured. He determined to make a positive move for himself and thank goodness that's exactly what he did.

BORN IN the suburbs of Washington, D.C. I attended the public schools in Washington, DC. As the fourth son born in my family. I was born in a poor family with seven sisters and five brothers. My father could barely get to work due to him being a seasonal worker. I bore the brunt of my father's shame as his son and grew up wanting to make things better for my parents; although I was just a child myself. My mother was taking care of us children and was always there. Money was scarce— it's just that sometimes sense and cents doesn't add up. We struggled as a family and did not rely on outside help; we did not wish to degrade ourselves. We had respect for family, privacy, and keeping it all in the family.

(Courtesy of Stewart C. Stevens, Sr.)

On some days we did not have anything to eat. There were days that we did not even have sufficient heating. Our home was heated with wood stoves and we had to have money to buy wood in order to stay warm. Icicles would hang off the roof and alongside the gutters for months until right around the time for spring and then they melted. In those days, winter lasted forever and it was much colder during this time in Marshall Heights. We did not have many buildings and no condominiums; we had nothing like that in our neighborhood to break the wind. When the hawk (cold winter wind) came down our street, we thought it was a hurricane. It was so strong and bitterly cold. It seemed just like the wind had come through like a razor into the siding of each house. There was no global warming either. We had outside water and we had to use pumps on the outside of the street to pump the water into buckets and take the water back into the house. We had to heat the water for bathing and washing dishes and we even had to use outside toilets. When it got real cold and the hawk came through again, the pumps would freeze up.

The reason I am telling this story is because I want everyone to know that in Washington DC during this time in history, this is the way we had to live because it was an all-Black, poor and underdeveloped community, and we could not afford to go anywhere else. We could not get out; the only way out was up and out. That's why I went out, out of school and flew up and out to other states and out to Germany. I flew out, and years later, the Queen flew in. It was historical for Queen Elizabeth II to have visited an underprivileged community in Southeast Washington DC. Queen Elizabeth II was the only dignitary that ever came into our community and it wasn't until years later during the Bush Administration in 1991 that First Lady Barbara Bush and the Secret Service escorted her to meet someone named Alice Frazier. Alice Frazier was a long-standing person within the community that remained in Marshall Heights, which was considered Ward 7 and one of the poorest communities. The Marshall Heights Community Development Organization developed and donated a new home to Mrs. Frazier at the age of 81. She lived on Drake Place SE. The Queen came to Shanty-town, and eventually the street was renamed to "Queen Stroll."

President Jimmy Carter, after his Presidential administration, had low-income homes designed and built in the poor community of Benning Heights, which is down the street from Marshall Heights. As a child, I attended the St. John's Baptist Church of Marshall Heights and was baptized. While in Germany as a young man, I was very homesick; I had never been that far from home and my spirits were down. One Sunday morning, while stationed at Fort Dix, New Jersey and listening to the radio in my barracks, an announcement came over the speaker from Reverend John H. Jackson, pastor of the St. John's Baptist Church of Marshall Heights and he said, "We all here at St. John's Baptist of Marshall Heights are praying for Corporal Stewart C. Stevens, who is now stationed in the military in Fort Dix, New Jersey." That really lifted my spirits and I was ready to move forward with my life.

On a brisk and windy morning, they rushed his mother to a local hospital in Washington, DC in 1938. Good morning, , said, the attending nurse. "You have a beautiful and healthy baby boy!" "How is my baby?" she asked. "Oh, he has a strong set of lungs and checks out fine! Your little tiger is ready to roar!" "Oh he must be hungry." "Yes he is and ready to eat and ready to get back in my arms!", "Thank you so much. Come on baby, I think I'll call you Stewart 'Calvin' Stevens. But Calvin is what we'll call you." "Hello honey how's my Baby and my little boy this morning?" said his father. "We are doing well, the nurse and doctor said everything checks out fine and he is a strong little Tike." ""Well, I'll be back tomorrow to bring my wife and little Calvin back home." "I will be ready about 11:00 after we check out with the doctor." "Sure thing, I will see you about 11:30 tomorrow."

In the following days, baby and mother came home from the hospital. "Oh Mama, Mama, it's so good to have you back home and where is our little baby brother Stewart Calvin? Let me see," said his brother. "Hey there little brother, we are sure gonna have some good time playing and running and you will like hanging with me and your big brother. "Yes, Ma'am I don't think he's going to change much." "He's a "Stevens" and we all have a strong resemblance." "You're probably right my son."

"Come along boys and girls and let's eat your oatmeal or you'll be late for school." "Your Daddy will walk you to school." "Oh Mama, it's so windy and cold outside." "Well, you have school and that comes first." "Tell you what, on Saturday, you can make paper kites and go kite flying since its March." "Yeah!" "That sounds like a wonderful idea. I sure wish Calvin was old enough to come." "Boys, little Calvin will join you in time." "My little team of boys," she said.

"Calvin, have you had time to go with your brothers to fetch some wood for the woodstove?" said his father. "Honey, little Calvin can't carry any wood, he's the smallest one of the boys", his mother said. "They're calling for a great snow tonight and he can at least learn by watching his brothers." "It's okay Mama, I am becoming a big boy and I can lift some wood too! Mama are you okay, I see that your stomach is getting fatter, I guess I'll have to stop saving my cookies for you," laughed little Calvin. "Oh baby, it's not because of your snacks "Wow!

I can't wait," said little Calvin. "I am also planning a birthday party for you so you will have two surprises in March." "Oh super!" Calvin said with a delightful sound. "You go ahead now and watch your older brothers. Within several years you can help with the wood, but not right now, okay?" "Okay Mama," little Calvin said.

On a cold January day the snow came falling down profusely. The children loved to go outside to make snow cream. "Oh Mama, can we go outside to make snow cream?" asked little Calvin. "No honey, not on the first snow fall; there are too many germs in the air." With no hot water during those times, the children also had to go to the water pumps to fetch water and bring back to heat on the wood stoves for bathing. "Boys, I want you to go get some water for bathing." "Oh Mama, it is so cold." "Well we need to bathe, cold or not, thank you very much! Now get moving." "Mama I wanted to lift some buckets of water too," said little Calvin. "Not yet baby, just watch for now and you will learn from the older boys." "Okay," I will, he said disappointedly and with a sigh."

As February rolled around, everyone was thinking and planning for the birthday party for Calvin. He was so excited about receiving all the attention from the older children. During the middle of March, Rachel started to also plan for the new baby. She had no idea during this pregnancy that the baby would be due around the same time as little Calvin. "Dear, she cried, I do believe something is happening and I must get to the hospital right way." "Are you sure Shug?" "Yes, it looks like we are doing it again!" "Oh Mama, what is happening?" cried little Calvin. "Well, Mama has to go to the hospital to just be checked out and I will be back later." "Mommy you know my birthday is tomorrow and I am so excited, can't wait for you to hurry and come back home," cried Calvin. As the evening grew later and night was coming on, little Calvin grew excited and yet fretful. Boy, I wonder what is taking them so long to get back, he thought. At about 12:45am, there was an alarming ring of the telephone. By this time, little Calvin had fallen asleep with anticipation and excitement for his birthday party tomorrow. "Yes, yes doctor," said his sister, "Okay, I'll let everyone know she said….I had better have a talk with little Calvin first. "Calvin, please wake up and come here to your big sister, I have something to tell you." As Calvin awakened he thought it was time for the party. He said, gee it's awfully early, has the party started? "No honey, but I have something to tell you." "Big sis what is it?" "Well Mama has to stay at the hospital and will not be back in time for your party. "Why?" He cried. "She just had your little sister and she was born on the same day as your birthday." "What's going to happen now, will I still have a party?" "No sweetheart, Mama has to get well and then we will have one for you. But you will have a little sister and maybe you will have a party together one day real soon." "Gee, I can't wait for that to happen," he said, with glee and sadness all at once.

"Good morning boys and girls," said the teacher. "We are here today and this is your first day of school. I would like for everyone to go around the room and introduce your name to each classmate." All of the kindergarten children were eager to start school on such a warm and sunny September morning. They were so excited because kindergarten was the beginning of independence from their parents. Each child was dressed with starched shirts and ties, and Buster Browns or Hush Puppies for shoes in those days. As the teacher gave the command, each child said his or her first and last name. Little Stewart, when he was called, began by saying, "My name is Stewart Stevens and my family calls me Calvin. This is my first day at John Carroll Nalle Elementary and I am glad to be here." They all clapped. Then everyone else chimed in and began to introduce themselves. The chatter was so loud that you could hear them outside the classroom. Ms. Brown quickly closed the classroom door as she raised her voice and hit the little red bell on her desk. "Time out everyone! Calm down, calm down class!" said the teacher. She hit the bell a few times and everything came to a halt. Eager to please his teacher, Stewart assisted with collecting pencils and papers at the end of the day. His teachers were amazed at how polite and helpful he was. He demonstrated a strong sense of courage and courteousness even at such a young age.

At the end of the day he would gather his beginner books and a lunch box with any leftover lunch and a snack. The John Carroll Nalle Elementary school, which was his neighborhood school, served milk and oatmeal raisin cookies each day for a mid-day snack. "Hey Stewart, you did not eat all of your cookies. Can I have one?" John said.

"No, I am sorry, but I am saving my snacks for my Mom," said Calvin. "You see, I like to share my cookies with my Mama because I love her and I want her to enjoy them as much as I do." "Wow! That is something. You must really love your Mama." "I do," said Stewart. "Hi Sis," said Calvin. "I missed you today, but is Mama home or out running a chore? I have something for her," he said while talking to his big sister. "Mama is here. She just came back from the store, Calvin." "You sure are a nice big sister, and you help Mommy out with us so well, I have a big hug for you too!" "I love you too Calvin," she said. Suddenly, Mama called out from the other room, "Calvin, I am so glad you are home; did you have a nice day in school today?" "Yes Mama, and I brought you something." "Oh my goodness," she said. "You are so thoughtful." "I thought of you today Mama and I wanted to surprise you." "You did surprise me," said Rachel. "You are just a little boy but so thoughtful. I hope to keep you around forever. Such a special and kind young man you are, but I know that one day I will have to let you try your wings and fly away." "One day you will make some young lady very proud, but I am in no rush to see that day," she smiled and laughed. Young Stewart had not realized what his mother was saying to him as a little boy, he simply said, "Yes Ma'am. I am not looking for that day either because if I could I would marry you. Can daddy and I marry you, he asked?" She burst out with laughter and said, "I don't think so but in my heart you will always be my little boy Calvin." "Children please settle down and help Calvin with his homework. Once he's through, turn on the old jukebox. He just loves music and dance. Or put on the *Amos and Andy* show. You all like that." "Yes Ma'am," said Big Sis.

A few years went by while Calvin began to grow and started getting closer with his older brothers. Playing, running, basketball, football, you name it. He always liked sports of every kind. Of course he had his chores to do, and with so many children everyone had various roles and responsibilities. It was time for another birthday.

The day had just started; it was a rather humid morning. Stewart is what they called him in school, both teachers and peers. He had awakened with the sound of cicadas chirping away. Stewart was so excited as he started out the door thinking of the spring activities generally held at the end of May, such as the May Day celebration

John Carroll Nalle Elementary School. He went to school as usual and had to go through sheer torture during his comings and goings. "Hello Calvin," said Mama, "My goodness what in the world is going on with your pants. All that red clay mud is coming into the house which keeps me cleaning and waxing the floors and besides when I wash it comes out into the water onto the others clothes." "Yeah, Mama, it keeps us going back and forth to fetch more water for more washing," said one of his brothers. "And it keeps me having to wash so much that I may have to ditch the pants and buy you all new ones. They should do something about these road conditions. Why they need to keep busting up the roads and messing up the community is puzzling to me. We'll just do the best we can. Maybe one day we can move from this wretched Community!" Once that's done, you can go out with your big brothers to walk the dog until your father gets home. He takes the streetcar and the bus. The streetcar line is from the Capital Transit Company and the bus has an odd number for the rush hour. Honey, I just can't remember the number but he'll be here soon." "Yes Mama. I love my little dog. He keeps me so much company, especially while I am waiting for Daddy to get home. I sure miss him," said young Calvin.

"Son, come on over and watch the baseball game with me. The Brooklyn Dodgers are on and Jackie Robinson is playing." "Sure Dad, replied, Calvin. I like seeing Jackie hit that ball and run!"

"I pledge allegiance to the flag of the United States of America, and to the Republic for which it stands, one nation under God with Justice and Liberty for all," as the class stood to the salute, the teacher said, "Hey there Stewart, how is everything?. I've noticed that you are a little preoccupied during your studies." "Oh I'm doing alright, Mrs. Overton," Stewart said. "It's just that I have my mind on some things concerning home life along with the messy road conditions and the way that we have to travel to get to school. It's all good and all, but I don't like having to go to this much trouble for a decent education and troubling home life. My dad doesn't work as much in the winter months, though, and then we have other problems...I keep telling my Mama that I want to have a job that pays me all the year round when I grow up. So I am trying my best get this arithmetic down so I can be something when I grow up. I see how hard we all have to chip in and all to help the family. I am so tired of dealing with so many things that don't seem fair. My father doesn't like for us to take handouts from anyone." "You know, Stewart, you are a very smart young man and you are really doing well in arithmetic, reading, and all other studies. I wanted to commend you for doing better than you know." "Are you sure, Mrs. Overton? I thought that I was not doing good," said Stewart. "Yes, you are doing very well! In fact, I am putting a word in for you to skip a grade. You will not have to go to the 5th Grade. You will be advanced to the 6th grade, and you will graduate." "Oh wow! I am so excited and my Mama and Daddy will be so surprised." "I am also putting you in charge of the class today so that when I go out of the room you will take charge of the class and give a reporting when I return. Would you like that?" "Wow! I sure would like that Mrs. Overton. I will let you know what is going on, you can count on me." "Thank you!" She said.

Calvin truly wanted to finish school as he stated on several occasions. Calvin was not proud that he had to make certain adjustments in his life to make a life for himself.

We can't choose our families of birth nor our parents; the parents can't choose and the offspring doesn't get to choose; it is a designed plan to whom and to where we are placed in life. It is a divinely-ordained assignment. All we can do is make the best life possible to afford a better way of living and these are choices! Choices are very important and they shape us; "Life Choices", "Cause and Effect" the same difference, we can choose! Although there are situations, when one has made right choices and still adverse actions follow. At least there will be Peace in knowing, the effort was put forth. Situations happen that one may have no control of and one can be free with no regrets.

That said, there was a Master plan of the One who orchestrated the life of Stewart Calvin Stevens Sr. He endeavored to do his best in school and he did it as far as the road took him. He had enough intuition at that young age to realize, "This ain't working","I must do something else."

Calvin then endeavored to enlist in the National Guard and if that meant acceptance of the fact that grade school wasn't working then so be it. His need for support which the military could and did provide by giving him that sense of Love & Belonging, Self-Esteem, Safety & Security, Physiological Needs and Self-Actualization (the desire to become the best that one can be; ironically that this is his motto). Maslow's Hierarchy of Needs teaches these basic principles. Now Calvin probably did not know this and not many do. It was once said, "You've got to follow Your Road". Hopefully, others can appreciate and understand that there are avenues to self-motivation and proceed into fulfillment of one's life.

The subconscious self knows of what each person needs! If this cannot always be found within the family structure, it can be discovered through a positive circle of peers, through networking, talking to those that have survived negative experiences or choosing a mentor that's understandably empathetic to your dilemma.

ALTHOUGH I WAS SMART enough to skip a grade and graduate at an accelerated rate, I did not do well in Junior High school as it was called during that time. We had to pay for tickets to get to school which put financial strain on our family of 13 children. My brothers and I had to pay for bus fare. If we had not been forced to bus outside of the community, and we could have walked to school as we had always done and things would have been better and more affordable.

I graduated from John Carroll Nalle Elementary School and went to Hugh Mason Browne Junior High School, which was named after Hugh Mason Browne, who was a civil rights activist and educator. He was a strong supporter of Booker T. Washington and the Tuskegee Institute. Browne was located on the East of the River on Benning Road, NE side of Washington, DC adjacent to Joel Elias Spingarn next to the picturesque Langston Hughes Golf Course. This entire area is known as a Historical District. I had to then take the bus from Central Avenue SE side in Washington, DC. During this time, tickets were required to get to school, forcing me and my brothers to buy tickets. I did not accept free lunch. I don't recall if there were any lunch programs for free or reduced lunch. Even in times when food was scarce, I was a stickler for not accepting handouts due to my father's belief system. He was a strong proud Black man with Native American roots who would not take welfare from the government. The segregation of schools did not work for us; it more or less worked against us.

We lived in a time where you could not go in the front door of some stores or places of business in Washington, DC. The H Street NE demographics were highly condensed with Caucasians. It was a European neighborhood and had better roads, schools, and vibrant entertainment and activities. It later changed to a predominately Black

Community. I did not live on H Street NE, we only lived there when I was born as someone told me. We had to move due to rent increase. I wasn't old enough to remember how it was then, but I see how it is now. I was the first to be born in Washington DC. The first five of us were born in Virginia.

The community we moved to right after my birth (Marshall Heights) was also a predominately Black community. Most families living in the community had a whole bunch of children and no one particularly cared about that community, which is better known as Marshall Heights. In every three-to-four room homes there were about 10-12 children. Due to the government digging up the streets causing broken pipes and red clay mud, conditions were unbearable. However, I made it! Streets with nothing but red clay mud left stains hard to forget, and nearly impossible to clean. The Red clay mud as red as brick had eased its way back into our homes from the soles of my shoes onto the wooden floors. Upon graduating from John Carroll Nalle Elementary and the day that I graduated, I carried my new shoes and wore my old shoes. When the time came to enter the building, I put my new shoes on when I was safely out of the mud and went on into school. I then put the old muddy shoes in a bag and hid them in the bushes somewhere until I got out of school only to put them on again for walking home. The Red clay mud as I can recall as if it were yesterday, left stains on the cuffs of my pants that so desperately needed washing or perhaps throwing out if they could no longer be worn. That Red clay mud is etched into my mind. I made it through, red clay mud and all, out of a bad situation. This became my steppingstone for future endeavors.

In the mugginess of the day brought on by the September sun that shone brightly through the clouds, Stewart and his brothers began to board the school bus headed for Browne Junior High School.

This was the first year he ever had to take the bus, which was public transportation. "Where is your ticket young man?" asked the driver. "How much is it?" said Stewart. "That will be .75 cents in the morning and another .75 cents in the evening," said the driver. "Well, it is three of us; me and my two brothers," said Stewart. "It will be the same for everyone who takes the bus," said the driver. The boys looked at one another with utter disbelief. "Man this is something," said his brother, "We had it made walking to school before." "Yeah, it would be great – all except getting past all the mud," said Stewart. "Yeah, if they would have let us go to Kelly Miller Junior High School, we could have easily walked there from our house." The bus stopped at each stop to pick up passengers headed for work, school, and other places around the city. The diesel fuel causing much upset to Stewart made his head swim. Suddenly, the bright sunny sky appeared with a gloom as Stewart felt his heart sink to his stomach. He held his stomach, fists clinching to his mid-section. "Hey little brother, is this getting to you?" said his brother. "Yes, I am feeling a little sick to the stomach." "Did you eat your breakfast, boy?" said his other brother. "Yeah just not as much because I am excited about the new school they just built, but I sure didn't know it would cause me this much trouble and be this much out of the way. I wish we could walk like we used to and kick around with each other before school. The air was cleaner, not like smelling gas from a public bus and besides it was more fun." "I know what you mean little Bro. But we'll make it like we always do. We are Stevens and we make it, yeah because we can take it!" Stewart reached up to pull the line with a bell to inform the driver they would be getting off at the next stop. The bus came to a halt, "Alright, those going to Browne Junior High, this is your stop." As they got off the bus, "Whew what a ride, but I sure feel better with the breath of fresh air" said Stewart.

"Are you guys alright?" "Yeah we made it," said Stewart, with a sigh Of relief. "Take care of yourself, baby brother, we'll see you after school, we'll get to the bus stop together." "Hey Stewart!" someone called out, "How are you today? Say, I remember you from elementary and boy you were something trying to take charge of the class and all last year." "Yeah , I like taking charge when I can." "You must have been Mrs. Overton's pet." "Seems like you are good at pleasing people, can I call you Mr. People- Pleaser?" "I like working and being nice," said Stewart, "if that pleases people then I guess you can."

"Hey brother, I sure got teased a lot today about being a people-pleaser. Some guy asked me if he could call me Mr. People-Pleaser. I can't believe that," said Stewart. "Well, I can, because you are nice, hardworking and like to look out for others," said his brother." "Yeah, let me meet this guy, Calvin. We'll make him think twice. His head will swim so fast once we get a hold of him. You know how Mama and Daddy taught us to stick together. You mess with one of us and you have to fight us all." "No, that's alright brother, I'm so afraid of what you might do to him," Calvin said. Hey guys, I may stop telling you things, I would hate to see him with a broken or bloody nose." "That might be best, Calvin, because we can't take someone badgering you like that." "Hey brothers, I love you guys, you're the best!" said Calvin. October had rolled around. The golden leaves of autumn had started to fall onto the ground with their burnished brown, golden, and orange shimmering colors. The hustle and bustle of getting to this new school was exciting, though. Warm October afternoons were especially nice as Indian summer was approaching. Unlike the elementary school, the courses in Junior High were divided into six, including Math, Science, Social Studies, History, Music and Arts, and Physical Education. Stewart was getting settled into his classes. The days seemed longer, although they got darker earlier. Catching the bus and all and wondering what to buy for lunch with the little cash he had to work with was becoming a bit of a challenge. The lunch prices were outrageously high. "Hey, what did everybody eat for lunch today?" said his brother as they boarded the bus going across the Sousa Bridge in Washington, DC. "I ate mostly snacks, but also an apple and a banana. I try to get some fruit in," said Stewart. "Yeah, me too, I had some old bologna sandwich that was expensive and the bread was very dry." "I had a sandwich too, but you know I got to have my Mary Janes and Squirrel Nuts," said his brother. "I thought Mama told us not to eat so much candy. Those Mary Janes and Squirrel Nuts will pull all your teeth out!" Stewart exclaimed with excitement. "Besides, dental work is very expensive, unless we wait for the school dentist to come." "Yeah, but my nerves are on edge, little Bro. Trying to get used to all of those different classes and in between classes hungry and catching the bus, I need something to snack on and oh, by the way I had a peanut candy bar. "Wow! What a name," exclaimed Stewart. "I don't know about you all, but on that note I think I am going to start an evening job perhaps next year," said Stewart. "After I get out of school, I am going to work somewhere. I think Mom and Dad could use a little help. We keep having more brothers and sisters. I noticed that November is coming around and Daddy's work usually slacks off in the winter season since he works construction. There is not much building in the winter with the ice and snow and all." "You seem to be very observant little Bro, and a planner." "Well, I was just trying to plan ahead, said Stewart.

Another year had gone by and it was now March, 1953. Stewart had just had his 15th birthday. The family was thriving and enjoying life. Stewart was picking up the share of his work when one of his brothers spread his wings and started his family. Stewart was a great young socializer and enjoyed attending teen parties and gatherings with cousins in Washington DC and some friends and cousins in Brandywine, Maryland. But most of all he liked sports, especially baseball star Jackie Robinson and tennis star Althea Gibson. Sitting down listening to Nat King Cole with his Dad was another favorite pastime. He grew to revere the music of Nat King Cole in years to come.

By the end of October that same year, Stewart had begun to think about working after school. "I think one of the bowling alleys is hiring and they pick up a lot of work especially during the holidays. In the winter, folks bowl when it's cold outside and they can't go to the beaches or outside activities. Yesterday, I went to the bowling alley to watch the leagues bowl. I like the feel of the bowling alley; there's so much excitement," he told his brothers. "The balls come up automatically, the place has a fresh smell, good eats – I can't resist!" said Stewart.

Lights glaring, bright red and green; shining lights permeated each section. The polished floors were so shiny that the glare of the lights' reflection seemed so cool. Music played and leagues geared up. There was so much chatter in the place. It only made me want to take part in the excitement. By being Black, and especially in certain neighborhoods, a person was prohibited from participating in such activities. Blacks could only set up bowling pins and watch from a distance while others played.

"Hey, Stewart, I noticed you voluntarily picking up the bowling balls, setting up pins, and putting them in place," said the man. "My name is Charlie Gentile and we have some evening openings here; I went through the applications and noticed yours but before I could call you—you are here acting as if we had already hired you." "Yes, Sir, I came directly from school to watch the bowlers play a game or two and I wanted to help by picking up the tin pins." "Well when can you start?" said Mr. Gentile. "I am not sure if I will have transportation," said Stewart. "That's no problem," said Mr. Gentile, "We will pick you up, just tell me where." "One question please, Mr. Gentile, what will I be doing?" "You are expected to pick up pins and that is all. No bowling except for Whites. You do understand, don't you?" "Yes of course," replied Stewart. "Please pick me up from Browne Junior High School, I am trying to surprise my parents and pick up money for the Thanksgiving and Christmas holidays." "So how are your grades, Stewart?" "Oh my grades are good; I skipped a grade and am very studios." "Is that right?" Mr. Gentile said. "Yep, that is right!" "Bring me a copy of your report card and I guess we can get started." "Yes and thank you Sir, said Stewart." "Sure," said Mr. Gentile, "Glad to have you on board!" "Perfect," said Stewart.

The next morning, Stewart eagerly ran out the door and caught up with his brothers to catch the bus. "Hey guys, I have a job after school! While I was there watching the league bowlers, voluntarily picking up pins and putting the bowling balls away the manager, Charlie Gentile, came to me and asked me if I would be interested in a part-time job. He had run across the application I completed." "What bowling alley is this, Calvin?" "It is the College Park Bowling Alley," Calvin said. "Oh, yeah? How in the world can you get out to College Park Maryland after school? That's going to be hard pulling that off, Calvin," said his brother. "Where there is a will there is a way," he exclaimed. "Surprise! I think they have a driver to drive the Bowling Alley van and it picks up. I will be setting up pins at the bowling alley. We cannot bowl as Blacks in this segregated area known as College Park, Maryland." "Well, you just be careful out there, you hear me Calvin?" said his brother. "Well, I'll be on my way to class. Thanks for the advice and I'll see you both this evening."

"Ah, November, November and this is the time to remember," as he thought to himself. The chill in the air and the aroma of firewood coming from the wood burning stoves made Stewart think more of the holidays. He walked ahead of his brother. "Let's see, Thanksgiving holidays, two birthdays one for one of my sisters and one for one of my brothers. I think I will surprise them all!" He whistled along as he rode the bus. "Hey little brother what are you up to?" "Hi Bro, don't you have a birthday this month?" "Yep, I reckon so," he said. "I can't wait, I'm almost a man – got a lot of thinking to do, though." "Yeah, me too," said Stewart. "Now I will be able to do so much with my extra money. Let's see," he said. "First save some for the holidays, buy me a new classic style college look sweater so I look super cool when going to school, give some to Mama since she may need a little for something she wants to buy. Gee, I guess I had better wait until I get my first paycheck," he thought. "I'm only making $10 a night."

"Whew, it was a long day today with all my thinking." "Hopefully, you'll keep your mind on your studies," Calvin. "You skipping a grade in elementary was great. You're the only one of us that has skipped a grade. You are smart and well-liked." "Thank you so much, I do believe I am smart enough to juggle things like going to school and working evenings and I'll be able to handle it. Besides, Mr. Charlie Gentile is sending a ride for me in a few days to start my new part- time job." "Have you spoken to Mom and Dad about this Calvin?" "No, not exactly," he said. I want it to be a surprise." "Would you all cover for me?" Calvin said. "Well, normally we would not, but for this we will, you never tell stories and are most honest and we understand what you are trying to do. We are trying to pick up some extra bucks too." "That sounds fabulous!" He proudly shouted for joy.

One December morning, as the cold freezing rain came drizzling down the window pain and a song he liked came on the radio, Calvin started singing in the tub as he normally does. He really liked music for sure. The hit was composed in the mid-50s. It was hard to get up out of the tub and as he took a quick bath. He thought, "I am so tired and I certainly do not feel like school today." He did push his way through. Although Calvin still awakened very optimistic about school, his new job and the thought of earning his own money and earning more money weighed heavily on his mind.

All things were considered and all things were not always agreed upon. Except a few things.

Calvin considered making a better life and its commendable of him for taking that giant leap of faith!...as it was often expressed to him. He realized the Bowling Alley gig was going nowhere. He saw the glaring, bright lights of red and green, he heard the nice music at the College Park Bowling Alley and the leagues gear up too, yet Calvin saw the big picture and decided that he wanted to go somewhere!

Calvin wanted to erase feelings of injustice whereas he was good enough to work at a major Bowling Alley during the mid-50's where whites could bowl yet blacks were the pinsetters and the same blacks were prohibited from bowling at this place of business in College Park, Maryland located right outside of Washington, DC, the Nations' Capitol? This moment of injustice weighted heavy on his mind even as a young teen—this he expressed to me in later years. This was his first reality of racism. What young adult would not want to bowl at a bowling alley that he immediately went after school to make a little change to support himself and purchase some fine rags as a teenager and have a little left to give his family, How cruel were these rules? Stewart had to catch a ride in a van to transit out to College Park, Maryland for a part-time job, yet no one would transit you back home nor to a place in close proximity to your home? Oh of course, I do recall him telling me that the van driver dropped him back to Mount Rainier at the bus depot. The fate of Stewart Calvin was at risk there in College Park a predominately white area; yet he persevered. This was around the time of the historical murder of Emmett Till.

At the thought of Calvin going somewhere, his mother and father realized too that this National Guard was a great plan, they considered it and they approved. It is a good thing for mothers and fathers to understand

and look at the odds stacked against a child or teen. Many people can or may be headed for trouble unless there is a positive role model or positive agenda in place. This goes for that era and so as for today, the same is applicable. Calvin went on into National Guard as he determined what he wanted ..... Great for all involved but mostly for him!

The National Guard Army and this entire experience worked out for the best. Calvin never had a record of any kind to neither make a shamble of his life nor did it interfere with the White House experience awaiting him in the near future.

I WAS GOING TO school and working nights at a bowling alley in College Park Maryland. A driver from the Bowling alley would come around to pick me up. Going to school during the day and working nights was very hard. One day I went to my mother and asked her to sign for me to go into the Army because I was not doing well in school. My mother did not want me to enlist. I told her I wanted to make something out of myself so I could help Dad. She said, "I will talk to your father." I then joined the National Guard.

Honk…Honk …Honk, "Calvin your ride is here to pick up for the Bowling Alley," said Mom. "Coming right out," Calvin hollered from his bedroom window. "Son, you know you are going to have to get to school and leave all that working after school alone. Your dad and I want you to put your education first and leave everything else to us. How you managed to hide all of this from me and Daddy, I don't seem to understand. And your brothers know better to keep such secrets! I'm not happy about all of this; I often wondered how you had money to give me, and I thought you maybe had been raking leaves or shoveling snow for some of the neighbors or one of your aunts in your spare time on the weekends." "Mama, sometimes a man has to do what a man has to do," replied Calvin. Overhearing the conversation, "Yes, but you are not a man yet," said his Dad. "I am the man here and you are the son. I really appreciate your thoughtfulness, but your Mama is right. This is the beginning of this school year and you're just a few months away

from turning 16. You only have a few more years before you graduate."
"I understand, okay, though let me think about how to handle it and
I'll let Mr. Charlie Gentile know," Calvin said. "Love you Mama and
Daddy; I'll see you later tonight. Keep the lamps burning for me!" He
hollered out.

"Get in the car Stevens, or we'll be late for setting up for the bowling
league tournaments. Mr. Gentile has been on edge. I know you are
juggling your education and working here, but you may have to make
some decisions real soon." "Yes, of course," he said. "I just had this
same drill from my Mom and Dad. But do me a favor, slow down and
get me there in one piece if you don't mind!" Calvin said.

Next morning, "Hey Evans, my Mom and Dad want me to focus
on my education, but I see the need to bring in a more substantial
amount than what I am making here," said Stewart. "My Mama and
Dad are right and you're right on it! I am only bringing in peanuts
compared to what I could make. I agree with education, but education
can come in the form of other means you know," said Stewart. "Like
what, Stevens?" Louis Evans said. "Well, like training; training for a
career, like vocational training, like military police training! That's what
I'm talking about." "Yeah, that would really lead to a career more so
than this place," said Evans. "But I'm not ready to give this job up yet,"
said Stewart. "So are you going to give school up?" Evans asked. "I do
believe that is an option. Although I can't give this up yet because my
Mama always told me *don't give up anything until you have another one
to go to.* She just doesn't know that I will have to give up school. Man
I think it's going to break her heart and I have to be gentle with her,"
said Stewart.

"Bacon frying, eggs and grits this morning"! Mama said. The aroma
of fresh coffee brewing filled the air. Calvin had awakened to pots and
pans clanking on the stove on this spring morning in April. He was just
shy of his 16th birthday in 1954.

"Good morning Mama. Good morning everyone! I feel good this
bright sunshiny day!" "Yes, I see son, come on and eat your breakfast.
I have not seen any report cards lately, and I was waiting to see yours!"
"Yes I know. I would like to discuss that with you and Daddy but
not right at this time. I would like it when just the three of us can

talk sometime later today. Daddy are you working late today?" Calvin asked. "No, I'll be home earlier this evening. I want you to come straight home from school and not work your part-time job this evening. Do you understand, Calvin?" "Yes Sir."

"Hi Mama and Daddy," I'm home, said Calvin. "Hi Calvin, have a seat son," said Daddy. "I'm glad we finally can meet up. You are just as busy as me Calvin and I thought it a good time to discuss your grades and your plans for the future." "Yes Daddy, I have been thinking a lot about my future, but not in school because I am not getting anywhere with my grades dropping and all. So I decided I would like to have a future with the United States Army. For that reason, I wanted to talk to you and Mama," Calvin said. "Oh no, said Daddy, don't tell me you want to drop out of school, son. You are a smart young man." "If you look at it this way I am not really dropping out of school, I am taking on another form of school, which is called training. Military training as a military police is what I want to do. It would provide for a great future and besides I can send some form of real money back home, not a few dollars here and there," said Calvin. "I do hope you both would understand. Mama, would you please sign for me to enlist in the National Guard? Please Mama, I am underage and I really need your help to pull this off. I need your approval with what I am trying to do." "Dear, what do you think?" "Well Babe, it's not like he is dropping out of school to stand around on the streets. He wants a chance to make a career for himself." "I guess you are right." Alright Calvin, bring me the forms and I will sign off." As Mama gave a look of concern she agreed and the tears rolled down her check as a stream of a river. "Excuse me, she said, I need a moment alone." Mama ran into the room and burst out in a loud cry, "Oh my baby, my baby, Lord please give me strength!" "Daddy, I am so sorry to have broken my Mother's heart, I love her, Daddy," said Calvin.

"It'll be alright son, just give her some time. Things will work themselves out. They always do," said Daddy.

FORT KNOX, KENTUCKY TO AUGUSTA, GEORGIA AND BACK

Fort Knox, Kentucky was a hard place. Basic military training or "Boot Camp". It was a hard place because it basically, as was called "Basic" and it was designed to sever a man from his mother and father. Boot Camp was designed to grow you up. This had to be mighty hard as one would imagine at the age of 14 or 15. A young man is still emotionally bonded to home and family; especially at this tender age. It's assumed that although Calvin had made this tough decision, that it was not an easy decision, and it was one that he could not renege on once signing up for it.. Yet the goal was to endure and make something of himself, to prove to himself first and foremost, that he could do better than "Marshall Heights" and what choices if any, did he really have?

Next step, Augusta, Georgia (Military School Graduated) what an accomplishment for Private Stewart C. Stevens to complete and graduate from Fort Gordon Military Academy and as a sharp-shooter! For the entire 16 weeks; he trained and he was determined. While thinking of his family back home and his lovely Marie. Surely she was an inspiration along with just knowing he was doing this for his own persona. It's a great thing to do something for yourself, to prove something for your own self-esteem. When proving it to yourself, no one, absolutely no one can tell you what you can and cannot do! Now, I'm saying this! I've did it, I've done it, I've lived it, and now I did many things for myself"....: "Now I knew what I was capable of and could do it for myself " is what Calvin said."

No hand-outs, no begging. It's nothing like self-reliance and self-confidence. Stewart Calvin Stevens, Sr. did it, he lived it, he was very self-confident and most importantly he taught this through his actions, which speaks louder than words.

And, Calvin came "Back" to his prize in Washington, DC!

AFTER JOINING THE NATIONAL Guard, they sent me to Fort Knox, Kentucky, for basic training. After basic training I went to Augusta, Georgia, for military police training. I did very well in military police training because I had always wanted to be a police officer.

Hut one, hut two, three, and four. On a cloudy morning the drill sergeant screamed out to the military troops. "Pick it up," he shouted. "Faster! Stevens get in line!" "Sir, Yes Sir," said Stevens. "Move it! Move it! March to your left, march to your right!" Stewart had started his basic training in Fort Knox, Kentucky. At the shout of the drill sergeant he was reminiscing about being back home with his family. He had written his Mom a couple of times already. She did not make it any easier, keeping him informed of all the happenings back in the community in Washington DC, which increased his longing to be home. He started to feel even more homesick after receiving Mama's letters. In each letter, his brothers and sisters had something to say. His eyes began to well up with tears after reading the letters. He remembered that he was doing this for them and to have better chances of having a solid career. "Hey, Stevens, what are you doing?" "Well, Sarge, I was just reading a letter from my family," Stewart said as he bent down to keep the Sargent from seeing him. The troops were only allowed to read their personal mail at night. "Stevens, you had better get that letter put away immediately. You are needed back in the field and stop all that crying, or should I call you Mama's Boy?" the Sargent screamed out! "Sir, Yes Sir," replied Stewart. How he wanted to give him something to let him know he was just the opposite of being a Mama's Boy. Stewart sure hated the fact of letting him see a speck of tears, which was considered a sign of weakness. Any temperature risings had to cool down at this point. The thermometer was definitely boiling over like a kettle of hot tea with a strong whistle ready to be served. "Oh dear," Stewart said. "Let me calm down! This is teaching me skills for dealing with things later in life and discipline over my emotions. I must be tough," he kept reminding himself. "If I blow it, it's all over," except him kicking me in the buttocks and hitting me in the chest was a test of faith.

Another five weeks went by with much of the same treatment. It was now time for graduation training and Stewart graduated from basic training, which he was proud of making it through. Stewart's next duty station was Fort Gordon Police Military Academy, located in Augusta,

Georgia. He was there for 16 weeks. Stewart Stevens qualified with the military police weapon after he made it, shooting a bull's eye at the range. During the graduation ceremony, the room was brought to order. It was so quiet you could hear a pin drop as the military instructors called out, "Private David L. Jones, next, Private Anthony R Wilson, next, Private Stewart C. Stevens." As Stewart went to receive his Certificate of Completion, he was so thankful and proud that he was gleaming, but only on the inside. He kept a straight face on the outside as he quietly walked back to his seat. "Hey Private Stevens, someone called out! Congratulations! Are you headed back to Mama?!" He just smiled. The next day the troops packed and boarded a bus back towards the train headed to Union Station. In this case, Stewart was headed back to Washington DC, to his hometown of Marshall Heights.

"Hey there, Calvin!" he was greeted back by all of his sisters and his brothers. There was so much excitement and smiling faces at the homecoming party for Stewart. They had a nice welcome home gathering. The neighbors in the community came together when they heard the news that Calvin was coming home. The community always supported one another. The party consisted of fried chicken, carved turkey, string beans, greens, mixed salads, tuna salad, and potato salad. It was all out of this world, made by some nice girl in the neighborhood. Cake and punch was served for desert.

"CALVIN, I MISSED you and boy do I have a surprise for you. I have a nice friend and her name is Janice Marie. She lives not far away and goes to Joel E. Spingarn High School. We go out shopping together and share a lot in common," said his sister. "After becoming acquainted with her, I would like to introduce you to her. All I can really say about her is that she is a decent girl. She's a little on the quiet and shy side. Anyway, her father is very protective and has spoiled her a little. You being such the good brother that you are, I figured you could spoil her some more. She goes by the name of Marie." "Well, well who's this pretty young lady? I'd like to make your acquaintance and so how are you, Marie? My name is Calvin and I would like to get to know you better." She looked into his eyes and he looked into hers and the eyes, which are the windows of the soul, reached down to the innermost parts of both their souls. There was an instant attraction and it was love at first sight (this is a non-fictional story, all truth as being told). He took her hand and they left to go walking away from the family, his and hers. They had much to talk about. The evening drew closer, they held hands and they talked a lot. "Calvin, I'm so proud to hear that you graduated from Military Police School." "Yes, Marie, I am so glad that is over with. I kept in touch with my parents and my sisters and brothers. We can get to know each other better during the 30 days that I am here," said Calvin. "Sure, Calvin, I am so glad that your sister introduced us," Marie said. "I was told that you are a real nice girl, and pretty too! I think we're going to hit it off," he said.

A couple of weeks went by, as Calvin went to her house and knocked on the door, Marie's mother came to the door, "Hi, you must be Calvin." "Yes Ma'am," he said. "May I please speak with Marie?" "Just a moment, Calvin," said her mother. "Marie, you have company," her mother quietly spoke. "Hi Marie, would you like to go for a walk?"

"Yes I would, just a moment. Let me tell my mother that we are going for a walk," Marie said. As they left, the two walked and talked for hours. "How about a movie?" he said. She replied, "I don't know, my father is kind of strict about me going out with someone I have not known for a while, especially a young man just coming home and on leave from the military. You'll be leaving in just a few days and I wouldn't want to get used to you and then have you not being here." "Well, Marie, Calvin said, we'll get to know each other and we can always write one another." "Sure, we'll keep in touch because absence makes the heart grow fonder," she said.

The next day before Stewart got up for breakfast, Mama was at the door. 'Hi Calvin, can we talk son?" "Yes Ma'am." "I noticed that you've been spending a lot of time with the young lady that your sister introduced you to." "Yes' Ma'am, I'm trying to get to know her because once I leave and go to Germany it will be a couple of years before I get back." "Sure son, I understand, but you all can write each other. You haven't had much time with your family since you've been back and we don't know when we'll see you again." Mama said. "Yes, that's right because he wanted to make something of his career and he has to keep a focus," said Daddy. "Calvin, go on out there with your brothers, you need to spend some time with them." Dad said. "Well, I really don't have too much more time left before I have to go." One of his sisters said, "Exactly!" "Yeah, I want to talk with some of my old buddies before I leave," Calvin said. As he walked up the streets before he left to meet some of the guys, he noticed Marie's house and someone looking out of the blinds, as he looked closer towards the blinds they closed. He then heard her mother say through the screen, "Marie, stop looking out the window, you're tear my blinds up!" "Yes Ma'am', replied Marie.

A few days had gone by and Calvin called Marie. "Hey Marie, I've been thinking that I don't have much time left so I would like to see you before I go." "Oh, that sounds like a wonderful idea!" she exclaimed. "You know Calvin, you are a wonderful friend." "Why thank you Marie, but you are going to have to give me a nice kiss before I leave," Calvin said and smiled.

"Hi Marie." It was just two days before Calvin was to leave and he called Marie for a date out on the town. "Hello Calvin," she said. "Are you still able to go out with me, he asked?" "Yes, I asked my father for permission to go with you and he said sure it's okay just be back and don't be out too late." "Oh, great, that's great, I'll be there to pick you up shortly," Calvin said. "Just be ready." The shiny yellow and black cab pulled in front of the house, and honked its several times. "Coming right out," she called "I was just getting my face powdered and lips prepped," Marie said. "You look as beautiful as a doll!" Stewart walked around and opened the car door for Marie. "Would you like to go to the Howard Theater to see James Brown and the Famous Flames?" "Why yes I would. I've never been to the Howard Theater before. Wow, Calvin you really know how to treat a girl!" she exclaimed with excitement." They had a wonderful time watching James Brown and the Famous Flames. When James Brown started singing, "Please, please, please, please and then draped his cape over his shoulders, Marie just went crazy! And she just jumped up with so much excitement. After the show, they stopped and went to Ben's Chili Bowl and then flagged a cab back home. The cab stopped a block away from Marie's house when Calvin looked at Marie and said, "Honey, when were you going to give me a kiss"? "Right now," she said. Marie grabbed Calvin and put her hand on the back of his head, leaned forward and gave him a big kiss. "Oh honey, I felt the earth move under my feet!" At that point Calvin knew that she was the love of his life.

"Honey, the moon is so bright tonight and the stars shining so brightly" he said as he walked her to the door. "I sure wish we had more time to talk, but since your Dad says not to be out too late, I'll just be grateful for the time we shared today. It's been a wonderful day." Marie knew that the next day would be the last day before Calvin would be leaving to depart for Fort Dix, New Jersey.

It was the next day. "Daddy, I'll be leaving tomorrow and I wanted to spend some time with you all," Calvin said. "Sure son, we were waiting for you to simmer down. With coming home and trying to connect to your friends and all, you've been rather preoccupied, but your Mom and I understand." "I'm really going to miss everyone for the next couple of years," Calvin said. "I'll write everyone and send you all some photos back home. I've been told that Germany is such a pretty place." Calvin said. "Calvin, I want you to continue to pray and write me," said Mama. "I have to send you off again, not as if I have any choice. There's always a special place in my heart for all my children. By you being away, gives me more to worry about." "Please don't worry, I'll be alright," he tried to assure her. In the back of his mind, he was still thinking of his love, Marie. Calvin loved Marie so much he really did not want her to see him leave because he knew he would cry. Calvin hugged and kissed Mama and shook hands with Dad and told them he would write them when he arrived at his next duty station. He then slipped out of the back door and went to catch the bus to take him to Union Station to get the train for Fort Dix, New Jersey. "Marie, Marie, my brother is leaving on the bus to board the train in Fort Dix." "Oh no, how can I catch up with him?" Marie said. "I must find a way to see him off." She quickly ran to the bus stop. As Calvin picked up his duffle bag and suitcase, a soft whimper caught his attention. Marie said, "Wait one minute Calvin, I have something for you." "What is it my love?" he asked. "It's a picture of me – something you can carry to remember me by. "Oh, isn't this beautiful," he said. "Your face is engraved on my heart, I could never forget you, but this picture helps me to have something to hold onto."

"Honey, I wanted to slip off without you seeing me because didn't want to see you crying. I am crying and I knew you would be crying and that makes it harder on the both of us. Marie please, don't cry, I'll be back, I can assure you of that." As Calvin hugged Marie, he could smell the sweetness of her perfume. Their embracing was so strong, mixed with the blending of their tears, hugs, and sweet kisses made for such a bittersweet moment in time. It was really hard to break away from such a feeling so powerful! "I'll write you every day. I promise." she said. As Calvin boarded the bus for Fort Dix, he waived, "Goodbye Marie!" And she waived, calling out "Goodbye Calvin, look for my letters. I'll be writing you soon!" They never saw each other anymore until his return from Germany. But photos and letters, prayers and the memories they shared kept their love alive for a lifetime.

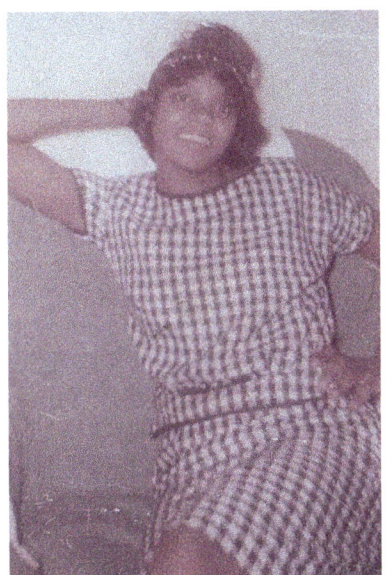

(Courtesy of Stewart C. Stevens)

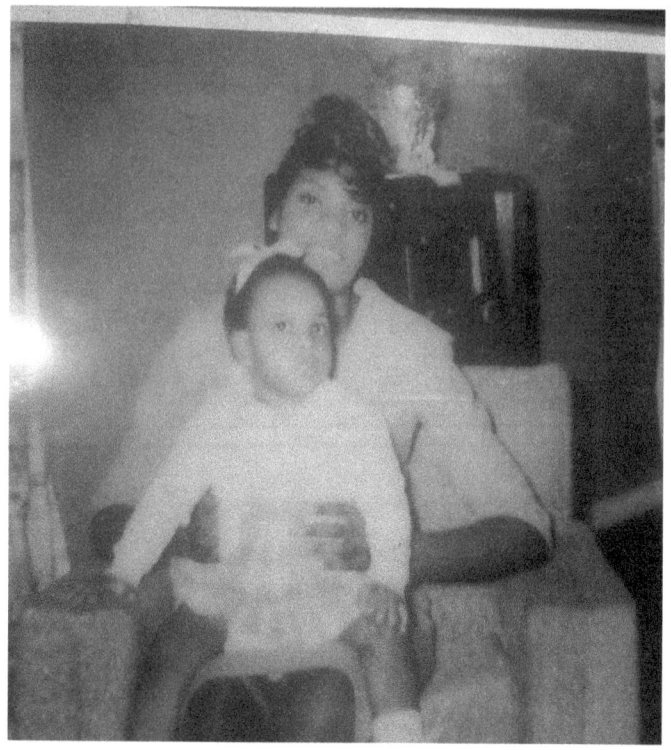

(Courtesy of Stewart C. Stevens, Sr.)

GERMANY

Next stop, Heidelberg, Germany!

The collision of the planes in Heidelberg, Germany caused emotional trauma for Stewart. It really was not expected according to Stewart. He was on his way to a meeting and "boom"! A sudden loud noise so unexpected arose out of nowhere. Debris of humankind fell all over the grounds. This was not his training of expertise having to go and gather up human remains. Corporal Stevens and other officers had received orders and they were to follow orders as instructed. While he was stationed at the 130th Station Hospital in Heidelberg, Germany, this incident was a most alarming and unfortunate event.

In speaking with my dad, Stewart C. Stevens Sr., he discussed how he often reminisced of this event as a youthful Corporal Stevens, Military Police (MP). This reminiscing was due to the trauma he endured. Unbeknown to anyone else, of course, his wife Marie was aware of this misfortune when it was shared by Calvin. It wasn't until later years, after the loss of Marie that he shared while out enjoying the day, during one of our ice cream ventures. How he loved ice cream! We would say, "I scream, you scream, we all scream for ice cream!" As one could recall, as a child he loved to go outside in the winter and make snow cream. Stewart never went into much depth of the effects of this event.

Unfortunately, he remembered the Germany experience throughout his life. He was never stuck nor did he allow it to hold him down from anything he wanted to accomplish. He was grateful for the time spent there in Heidelberg.

(Courtesy of Lynetta Stevens)

In Memoriam of a Life So Valiantly Fought for
And So Deeply Missed. Your Spirit Lives On.
Stewart C. Stevens, 1938-2023
U.S. Army 529th MP Battalion, Germany 1956-1960

Stewart later shared of his many buddies he had in Germany and a person he thought to be a friend of whom stole his duffle bag. The duffle bag had many letters from his girl, Marie, yet he never recouped the treasurable love letters. Marie had all of his love letters to read and re-read during the years. While Stevens was stationed in Germany prior to engagement and during his marriage to Marie, his family of origin took a photo and sent it abroad. His youngest brother was holding up the photo (a photo within a photo) of his big brother, Corporal Stevens; as a gesture of pride! Marie was all dollied up; Marie's father kept her dressed to the tee! The picture showed his girl Marie standing right there showing support even when the White House was nowhere in sight. My being the first and the tender age of about 3 three years, (Daddy was in Germany in the first few years of my life), I relished in the young love of my parents…before life became so busy and life changes…I have so many memories of them in their youthful love and especially so when I listen to oldies. They really loved each other. I'll never forget their young love.

Marie on Top Left

(Courtesy of Lynetta Stevens)

During our conversations, Stewart shared several topics of his upbringing. What was really caring and naturally not his responsibility to care as he did, (since the parents are to protect and provide for their offspring), yet it's factual that young Stewart sent money back to his father and mother to help financially with their children….his siblings. After joining the U.S. Military, and as a very young middle son, Stewart Calvin took on this responsibility (as a form of "Parentification") that was unduly burdensome. He never complained. Later as he matured and married, his priorities shifted to his wife and family and understandably so.

Stewart Calvin was a great dresser too! Even in his early years and with little cash, he still managed to find a way; more than likely once he had started his job at the College Park Bowling Alley. Stewart had a "Debonair" style (as referred to by many) and dressed to impress on into his later years.

WHILE ON 30-DAY MILITARY LEAVE before going to Germany, I met my first love, my only love, Janice Marie. My sister introduced us to one another. We fell in love and the first time she kissed me I felt the earth move under my feet. The young lady was a very decent girl, and she would not let me do nothing but kiss her. When I had to leave and go overseas to Germany, I could not stand to let her see me cry so I slipped out of my house and went to catch the bus. But my sister told her that I had gone. She met me at the bus stop. Just before the bus came, I looked over my shoulder and there she was standing there crying and she asked me why would you leave without telling me? I told her that I didn't want to see her cry although she was crying anyway. We kissed and I had the same feeling that I had the first time she kissed me. She told me that she was going to miss me too. She told me she would write me every day and she did just that. She wrote me every day as promised. I also received lots of letters from my mother.

I went to my Financial Officer to request that they draft a Class E Allotment to send a portion of my pay back to my family in Washington DC while I was overseas. When I went to Germany I was one of the youngest guys in the 529th Military Police Battalion.

(Courtesy of Stewart C. Stevens, Sr.)

(Courtesy of Stewart C. Stevens Sr.)

That is where I spent nine months and then I was sent to the 130th Station Hospital. This was a historical hospital where General Patton died. I was told he was hurt and the paramedics brought him to the 130th Station Hospital, which was before my time. General Patton had died in Heidelberg, Germany. Heidelberg was one of the prettiest cities in Germany because while the war was going on the troops stopped short of coming into the city. The site of the beautiful Castle is so picturesque. The closer you got to Heidelberg, you could see bullet holes in the bridge as a result of the war between the United States and Germany ending. This site was visible even before actually coming into the city. One day we had got the message that two airplanes had collided in mid-air and they were loaded with officers on the way to some meeting. The 130th Station Hospital Military Police, to which I belonged, was sent out into the fields where the planes crashed. I had to help gather up the dead body parts. I was in the field trying to write as best as I could because the troops didn't have much time to write.

POST GERMANY

Stewart knew Marie from the young age of 15 or so and then they connected as sweethearts later around 17. He always knew of her though as the girl that lived across the street. Initially, Marie was a family friend. One of his sisters and Marie were around the same age. Calvin's admiration for Marie's homely skills of caring for her brothers and sisters was very impressive. The familiarity of duty and responsibility was a common-bond between the two enabled their fondness to grow; the physical attraction was evident. This was the kind of woman that he wanted as the mother of his children.

After Germany, getting back to life was a bit hard. He was glad to go to Germany…it was like getting away from home and taking a trip that he would never have been able to take otherwise. How about that! A ticket out of Marshall Heights.

There was so much tension in Washington, DC due to racism that he was elated to go. Almost like getting out of fog, getting into clear fresh air and returning back to much more fogginess again. Or it appeared to be worse, simply because you were out of the denseness. When returning back to DC, this fog finally hits you much harder than before. Being back in the States was the real deal!

Germany had some of the same but mostly among its own people. Stewart did not experience racism from the German people. He shared, that there was subtle racism in the (American) military between black and white. Corporal Stevens holds the camera and takes a photo of his military friends that he walked back from a meeting.

It was so pretty there in Germany and the people of Germany were not prejudice of skin color nor skin tone. The foods were tasty, the German Ketwurst with sauerkraut, Reuben sandwiches, beers and lacquers, sitting and listening to nice music and entertainment (of course when he had *time) was a nice pass time and a way to unwind while smoking a zigarett and thinking of his girl. The customs were different. Yet there were some depressive areas of Germany. However, the chance of being away presented opportunities to see how other people lived.*

Corporal Stewart Stevens getting away from his town of birth was a good thing. This enabled him to mingle with people of other cultures; even later at the White House. He never let previous injustices in life get in the way.

("Steve" at White House with some staff and friends)

When it came to the White House this was a plus. The White House Baker, Mr. Roland Mesnier (A Switzerland descendant) and Stewart hit if off pretty well! Mr. Mesnier was so kind to our family with the baking and gifting of Gingerbread houses that he sent us during Christmas.

During several of Stevens book events and when reuniting again at Mesnier's birthday celebration in 2019, they were happy to embrace once more as Mesnier invited him up on the stage at the Willard Hotel, Washington, DC as recalled (Lynetta). No one knew this would be the last time that either of the two would embrace. Mesnier and the White House

Historical Association sent an invite to Mr. Stewart "Calvin" and Lynetta Stevens. She drove Stewart there and they both enjoyed the occasion!

Oh well Corporal Stevens leaving Germany to head back home, "Blah". The only good thing about it...it was his birth country, the United States of America and he was able to get back to Marie. It was not completely visible at that time that he would end up loving his country as much and working for the U.S. White House! He once told me, "There's no other place like home".

So yes, there's no place like home. Once Stewart finally realized he was back home, he was a little devastated at the conditions of not being able to land a decent profession....one that he really wanted that of a "Police". Since he was an MP, Military Police, why not? The second injustice as a young man after the military. The Washington, DC police force was only hiring whites for these positions.

After the racial injustice of the Metropolitan Police Department kept him from becoming an MP –Metropolitan Police here in Washington, D.C. and prior to the White House, Stewart did briefly work as a Bus Boy waiting tables and which he tells the story of how he picked up the tips that the waitresses were supposed to get. He didn't know...he says that he *assumed that the tips were for him. This is hilarious! He gave the tips back to the young ladies and left that gig for washing windows in residences throughout the metropolitan area. To Stewart's dismay, he was never accepted after passing the police exam. Yet he elaborated on it only briefly, especially since the White House position is where he was destined for. No one did what he did! He liked being unique.*

WHEN I RETURNED HOME from Germany, we met and talked about getting married. I told Marie that as soon as I had gotten a good job, we would get married. I knew that God was going to bless me with a good job and he did. They had one Black Police Department and a Black Fire Department. I did not know that when I had taken the test for the Washington Metropolitan Police Department they were not hiring Black men for that particular station. I had to put my name on a long waiting list at the Black Police Station and the Black Fire Department. No one told me that this was a waste because they were not integrated at this time. Nevertheless, I had taken a test for the Fire Department and the Police Department and passed both tests. There was a lot of racial discrimination in Washington DC around this time.

When I was not hired by the Police Department, my brother and I started a window washing business that was hard work due to so much competition from larger established companies. We subcontracted work from larger establishments by taking on some of their projects. I purchased an engagement ring and proposed to my sweetheart Marie and we were married. We were so much in love that I could not afford to wait until I got that special job. We were ready to start our own family.

"Morning, morning everyone, some of you will pass the exam and some will not. We'll mail your results in about a week. Those of you who did not pass, just come back in a few weeks and retake the police examination. Be here bright and early as the test starts promptly at 8:00 am," said the instructor.

"Hey Mom, did I get any mail today? I'm expecting results from a few of the tests I took." "What kind of tests Calvin?" Mama, said. "I took one for the Police Department one for the Fire Department," said Calvin. "I hope you passed Calvin. Can someone check the mailbox, please?" she hollered out. "Yes Ma'am," said his sister. Seconds later, "Yes Mama, Calvin has a few pieces of mail." "Thank you, honey. Calvin, you have a few pieces of mail." "Well open it son, open it!" cried his Dad. "For Pete's sake, what are the results?" As Calvin quickly tried to open the mail, he was going to tear the top off the envelope. Someone called out, "Not like that, use this letter file so you won't tear it up and then you won't able to share it with all of us! We want to know too big brother," his little brother was just as eager to find out what was in the envelope. All eyes were bright and stared as Calvin opened the first envelope. This is from the Police Station, he said as he read: "*Congratulations, you have passed the District of Columbia Police Certification. You may or may not be contacted within the coming weeks. Although we have several vacancies we are not hiring Negroes. Please contact the Hiring Authority Department for further information.*" "What?" Said Calvin. "I don't believe this." "Keep your head up son and just contact them within a few weeks. You've got to get a position with them; after all you have Military Police Certification," said his Dad. As Calvin opened the next letter from the Fire Department; he was enthusiastic than before. His heart was set on being a policeman, not so much a Firefighter. Although he took the exam as an alternative, he wasn't really trying to put out any fires! The brothers and sisters had lost their zeal when watching him open the next letter, which read: "*Congratulations, you have passed the District of Columbia Firefighter Certification. You may or may not be contacted within the coming weeks. We do not hire Negroes.*"

"Well, I'm ready to work and do something, I got my girl and we are planning on marrying." "Hey Calvin, I was wondering if you wouldn't mind working with me until something in your field comes along, said his brother Walter. You've been in the Army and over in Germany where people treat you like something and I know you didn't enlist to come back home to all of this discrimination, but for starters, I'm heading up a window washing business. It will be our family- owned business. I went downtown and paid for all of the licenses and certifications for starting a small minority-owned business with a government agency." "I'm not too proud to learn another skill and who knows where it will land me!" "Okay then, we'll get started right away." "I'm getting married and before I do, I need to put some more money away and get my girl some rings," he said.

Next morning, "Hi, I've been looking for that special ring for a very special girl. My girl doesn't like anything that is too big but a precious diamond that is more on the dainty side. She's dainty and has small fingers." "Sure young man. What's the special lady's name?" "Her name is Marie," said Calvin. The jewelry store manager started singing Maria, Maria, and Maria. "Oh, I saw that movie, was it West Side Story? Yeah that's it. Only her name is Marie you know, French for Mary or Maria?" "Well I wish you two the best of luck young man. Okay, let's see, these are nice. Do you think she will like this set?" "Oh yes, Calvin said. This set looks more like her!" "Okay. I'll put them on a payment plan for you. Just stop by every week and pay on them. The bigger the down payment, the sooner you will have them." "I will pay cash for the engagement ring because I want to propose to her immediately. If you could, please put it in a small box, I'd like to surprise her you know. The other one, which is the band, I'll keep paying on that. Don't worry it won't take me long to pay it off. We're not wasting a lot of time. Marie has been very patient and I would not want to keep her waiting for too long. There are plenty of hungry cats out there waiting for my little kitten. She's really sweet."

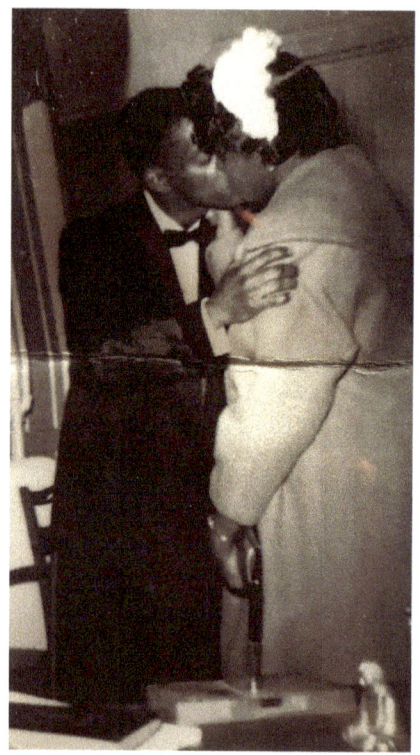 

(Courtesy of Stewart and Janice Marie)

PART II:

WHITE HOUSE HERE I COME

STEWART "CALVIN" AND JANICE "MARIE"

Stewart (Calvin) and Janice (Marie) had an enduring marriage for many years. Marie made the house a home. Without her strength and fortitude of loving and caring for her husband and children this could not have been possible. He wanted to ensure that he could provide for his wife and he did his best to provide a lavished home, family car and looking nice and their children well provided for. As a father, he wanted to give much because he didn't have much growing up. Each Christmas Calvin and Marie gave the best, the Bells and Whistles to their children. He wanted his children to have much of what he lacked in his childhood, The love and time they provided was commendable. If Stewart couldn't give as much time once working for the White House and providing financially, Marie evenly balanced and gave much more time as a stay-at-home Mother. Just her being there for her children and her husband physically and emotionally meant everything. We never had a babysitter. Both time and money are equally important!

She was the wings behind the man that worked so effortlessly putting in all the work hours in the manner in which he did. Stewart "Calvin" started at the U.S. White House long after they were married during the Nixon administration; as we know, President Nixon only served one term. In the early years of their marriage, he worked by washing windows in residential homes throughout the Washington DC area, now called the "DMV".

Stewart Calvin was a great provider throughout his life to his wife and family; Marie was a great provider too! He undoubtedly would not have been the person he had become during his White House position of Chandelier Polisher Specialist. As a middle child of 13, he grew up rather fast since he left for the National Guard Army in as early as the 7th grade. Marie grew up working in her family of origin as the eldest while assisting her mother with younger brothers and sisters. At a tender age, Marie cooked meals for the family and then later as she matured, assisted with her father's fence company. This all kept her busy along with attending school. Marie, attended John Carroll Nalle Elementary, Kelly Miller Jr. High and Spingarn High School. It was the kind-hearted and patient Marie that understood Calvin's work ethic as it was familiar to that of father. Her father designed and built his own home in the Nations' Capitol as his business took off.

Marie on the other hand, was an excellent cook, very gifted in writing and had a great talent as a seamstress! As it is recalled, "My Mother made so many of my clothes and they looked as if a they were professionally made!. She made us matching outfits on several occasions." McCall's and Simplicity patterns were for mother and little daughter (early to late 1960's prior to Dad working the White House). Being 17 years apart, Mommy and I shared the same bed while Daddy was in Germany. Since I never slept in the crib as a baby, our mother-daughter bond" formed very early. It is recalled, Marie shopping at the Jumbo Food Stores and she collected "Top Value Stamps" in the early 1960's. Once those books were filled up, we could purchase anything such as the Bone China Collection sets. To this day, (vintage collectibles) a set of Bone china with such a rare and pretty floral design!"

Marie was a great coupon saver and this of course helped with managing the family budget when combined with weekly items on sale. She may not have been the "Bread-Winner" but she was a "Bread-Keeper, while managing the dough!". Marie found time to volunteer at her children's elementary school, by the way it was John Carroll Nalle. This was the same school that she and Calvin attended as children. The first 3 children attended this as their elementary school. She rotated with other parents, bringing juices and cookies to school as snacks. She really liked children and they liked her. She went on several school trips as a chaperone with the children. On occasions, she taught Sunday school as a back-up teacher.

*It was Marie's enduring love for her husband that kept the home light burning long after hours, where as many couples had turned in. She would not go to bed until she was satisfied that her husband had returned home safely and they could have that cup of tea with honey and lemons together. Stewart in turn would always bring in delights from the White House State Dinners as some butler provided as a kind gesture. Marie even assisted with letter writing to several of "**STEVE's**" (his White House Brand name)* supervisors. The decision of her being a "home manager" was strictly by choice to care for their children and home. Marie sure could throw down those delicious home-cooked meals for her family and to her husband's delight. Back in the mid-1960s, Marie had an IHOP menu prior to IHOP. At times some evening meals were bacon, eggs, pancakes, French toast, home fries. Everyone loved it!

Prior to her support for her husband, Marie or Janice as is her first name, was very much in love with Calvin as they typically called one another by their middle names. Again, this was generally a custom of that era. Marie displayed love, affection, and support way back when and especially upon Calvin enlisting into the US Army. Letters were sent to Calvin every day and he wrote her as often as time would allow —in between Boot Camp, Fort Knox Tennessee, Augusta, Georgia and of most assuredly in Heidelberg, Germany.

They enjoyed the times they spent even after retirement while in one another's company. They were truly a team!! And you had better not mess with one of them; or you had to deal with the other one!!

Along with his venturing out, U.S. Military, the companionship and love he shared with Marie, and The White House experience, gave Calvin this euphoria. And in that order is how it was done.

HOW I GOT THERE

The love for Calvin and Marie and their story has been the driving force; the respect for his work ethic and craftsmanship of the Chandeliers and love for Calvin (Dad) the work ethic, tenacity, and love for how Marie (Mom) provided a loving home atmosphere. The appreciation of (Mom) for keeping the family together when times were bumpy due to meager earnings before the White House. Her sticking in there when Stewart Calvin worked in big homes washing windows throughout Washington, DC has been such a motivation.

How he got there? Good question. It was not by chance, happenstance, luck, familial relation (as some White House staff were related) nor education. Education is education and Genius is genius. It was a miracle and his genius of making a lasting impression by showing off his workmanship on the very first day!

Besides, Stewart asked for more work once he finished the task of cleaning the windows. He actually requested to do one of the Chandeliers! When Stewart Calvin announced that he had been offered a job there, Marie was elated!

AFTER GETTING MARRIED, OUR family started to grow. My brother and I were taking on more subcontracting jobs and this is how we got to work at the New Executive Office Building. To tell you the truth, there is no sound explanation of how I got there because there was a gentlemen standing there by the ladder that did not know me named Charlie Rotchford. I've had people of the White House Staff to ask me how I got there. I was not recommended for this position. In most cases people that have worked as White House staff had to be recommended by someone they knew as close friends or family members. In my case, I knew no one, no friends nor family members that ever worked for the White House. As a matter of fact, I was born, raised, and lived in the Nation's Capital and had never visited the White House, not even after returning from the military. So, I choose to believe that I was placed into this position as appointed by no one on this earth but rather a higher force. A man with my status, born in a poor family, with limited education had been to Germany and traveled a bit, but had no idea I would end up at the highest place such as the White House. And to prove it, once my tenure had ended, the position of Chandelier Polisher and Window Washer vanished. I never thought I would meet some of the most important people in the United States of America and from around the world. There's just no way I should have landed there except it was God-sent. I've met Presidents, Emperors, Queens, Prime Ministers, Pope John Paul II, movie stars, entertainers and other important dignitaries.

While working at the New Executive Office Building on a window-washing job, a gentleman by the name of Charlie Rotchford approached me for work at the White House and the rest is history. Charlie Rotchford was the Building Manager in that area. He talked to me and asked me if I wanted to work at the White House. I replied, "Yes Sir!" He asked me if I had ever been in any trouble and I told him, "No Sir." He asked me if I had been in the military and I told him, "Yes Sir." Then he told me to come to his office in the Old Executive Office Building. Mr. Rotchford gave me some papers to take home and bring back the next day. I came back the following day with the papers and he issued me a temporary pass until I could be cleared by the Secret Service to work at the White House. Once I had a temporary pass, I had access to the White House. He wanted me to meet a gentleman by the name of Mr. Wilson, who was the window washer at that time and was not doing a very good job. So I started washing windows. I was doing a good job because I had been washing windows for years. After working there for about six months, I went to Mr. Rex Scouten's office for a meeting and told him that I had been washing windows for some time and there wasn't any work to keep me busy. He looked up at me very surprised. I told him that the chandeliers were very dirty and I had experience in cleaning chandeliers. He said to me, "These are very old chandeliers, but I'll let you try and see if you can clean one. The painters put up scaffolds and I proceeded to clean the chandeliers in the cross hall. The Chandeliers were so dirty they actually looked as if they had mud on them. After polishing the Chandeliers, the word got all over the White House about how good the Chandeliers looked. Some said that the chandeliers had never looked that good before. Actually, I had never counted how many chandeliers there were in White House because there were so many I did not have time to count them all. I probably would have stopped cleaning them had I known exactly how many there were.

While working at the White House in the role of what I was hired to do, they requested me to perform multiple other tasks such as working as a carpenter's helper and assisting the office of Operations. This included set up and breakdown of the podiums and stages and other duties. One other prestigious job that I enjoyed was working at the State dinners and events that hosted several entertainers. Over the years, during the State dinners, I became acquainted with Mr. Eugene Allen, the White House Butler from the start. We became good colleagues and good friends. There were many State Dinners during my tenure at the White House. Some performers I had the pleasure of meeting during these events were entertainers like Sammy Davis Jr., Frank Sinatra, Muhammed Ali, Gladys Knight and the PIPs, Aretha Franklin and a few others. Some dignitaries that visited the White House were Mr. Al Sadat, the President of the Arab Republic of Egypt and Mrs. Al Sadat, Dr. Bruno Kreisky, Federal Chancellor of the Republic of Australia, Margaret Thatcher, British Prime Minister (referred to as the *Iron Lady*), Pope John Paul II, Nelson Mandela, the President of South Africa and several others. On the occasion of the signing of the Egyptian and Israel Peace Treaty in Celebration of Peace, the Egyptian Trio, which consisted of Omar Khorshav, Gamal Saidraheem, and Mohammad Helmy Ameen were musicians who played during the celebration event.

In my possession from several years ago are menus of what was being served. Some things that were being served at the Egyptian and Israel Peace Treaty were Columbia River Salmon in Aspic Cheese Straws, Roast Sirloin of Beef, spring vegetables, Hazelnut Gianduja, Mousse, Petite Fours and Demitasse. For the event in Honor of his Excellency the President of the Arab Republic of Egypt and Mrs. Al Sadat, the entertainer was Pearl Bailey, who was named as the US Ambassador of Love by President Nixon.

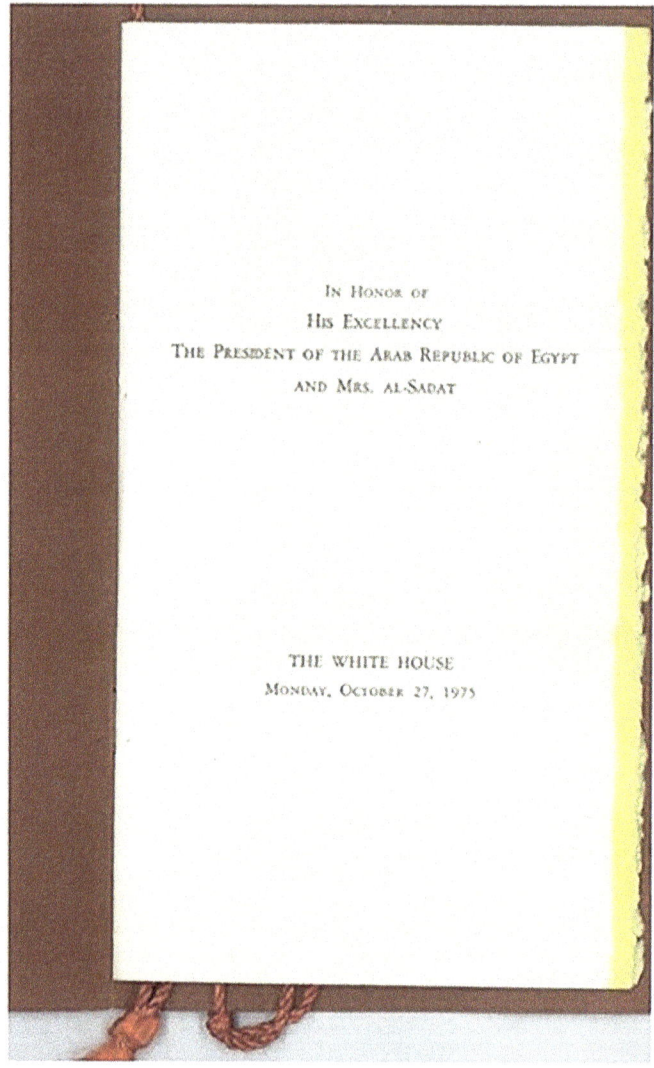

IN HONOR OF

HIS EXCELLENCY

THE PRESIDENT OF THE ARAB REPUBLIC OF EGYPT

AND MRS. AL-SADAT

THE WHITE HOUSE

MONDAY, OCTOBER 27, 1975

(Courtesy of Stewart C. Stevens Sr.)

While working during these events I was really doing my job. I spoke politely to each entertainer and dignitary but I was unable to get any autographs based on ethical policies of the White House. However, it was really nice seeing them in person. My attire when doing my job washing windows and polishing Chandeliers was informal. Attire on the days that I was supposed to work at the dinners was formal because as a coat checker this was the requirement. Working closely with Mr. Eugene Allen, the Butler, was a pleasure. I worked with The "Butler" for over 25 years during the White House State Dinners and Events.

On a rather bleak and cold morning, Calvin walked out of his house with his lunch. "Honey, don't forget your lunch I made you. Tell your brother I said hello," said Marie. "Thanks baby, I will." Bam! As Calvin got in the White pickup van and slammed the door tight, the old van was a model Ford used to carry work materials for window cleaning and washing projects. "Good morning brother, how's the family and all?" "Mine is fine. Another child on the way and all," said his brother. "I hope we can pick up some more business up there on Georgia Avenue, NW and on into Silver Spring, Maryland." "Yes, me too," he said. "Oh by the way, my wife said to tell you hello." "Well, where are we headed?" "We are headed up to Chevy Chase and Kensington today. They have really large homes and estates out that way. Say Calvin, I have a few contracts with some federal agencies and I'm feeling that this would be more stable for you and me and there wouldn't be so much riding around. What do you think bro?" "I think that sounds fantastic! When do you think we can start?" said Calvin, "I'm all for it." "I have to wait for a call to come in from one of the people I am working through called a hiring agent and liaison that would help to get us in. I think they call him a Contract Specialist through the General Services Administration. I had to place a bid on the project and there are a few other bidders. If our bid comes in the lowest, we probably will be contacted." "Wow, that is great news," said Calvin. The telephone rang loudly and abruptly as they were in the middle of a project. "Mr. Stevens, this is Mr. Grays, I'm calling to inform you that your company was approved for the window washing bid." "Why thank you. I'll let my business partner know." "Thank you Lord! And a call was quickly made a call to his brother informing him of the good news. "Hi, Calvin, I wanted you to know that they accepted our bid." "That's great!

"That's exactly what I said: That is Good News!" "I'm ready so when can we get started?" asked Stewart. "Well, he said we can get started next week. Okay we both can let the wives know," said his brother. "I'm sure their faces will light up like Christmas Trees!" "Yes Siree," said Stewart. "Alright then, I'll let Mr. Grays know we are accepting this offer and I'll pick up some more supplies." "Yes of course. Thank you, we'll be in touch before then though," said Calvin. "Yes, we will!" said his brother."

The following week came around and the day was finally here. "Good morning Calvin, you look well-rested," said Walter. "I am; I went to bed early and I am so eager, this is like a new start. Something secure and exciting and we'll be working every day of the week, not on as needed basis and on commission like we used to," said Calvin. "Yes," said Walter, "because the bills pile up every day and we need to be sure we can make the grade, cause empty pockets don't ever make the grade just as Billie Holiday said in the song *God Bless the Child That's Got His Own*," he said. "So here we are, the Commerce Department."

Day in and day out at the Commerce building, the Stevens brothers worked hard washing windows. They were working up a heavy sweat when someone came by to inform them that a new contract would be up for bid at the New Executive Office Building. They were elated. This may be more promising they both said simultaneously and looked at each other and gave a high-five as they exploded with laughter. They applied of course, and the bid was offered to them so off to the New Executive Office Building they went.

The New Executive Office Building was a nice Red brick building. It was newly built and much more appealing than the Old Executive Office Building also called the "Eisenhower Office Building."

"Good morning Mr. Stevens, my name is Charlie Rotchford and I am the building manager of the New Executive Office Building. I wanted to introduce myself to you." "Hi, nice to meet you Mr. Rotchford. "Stewart (as he was called by the staff at his new job) we have some availability at the White House. Would you like to work at the White House? Do you think that is something that you would be interested in?" asked Mr. Rotchford. "Oh! Yes Sir! I would," said Stewart. "Well, have you ever been in any trouble before Stewart?" No Sir, said Stewart. "Do you have any military experience?" "Why, Yes Sir I have military background. "I'd like for you to meet with me in my office over in the New Executive Office Building then," said Mr. Rotchford. "I have some papers for you to take home and complete. Bring them back tomorrow and we can meet again." "Thank you Mr. Rotchford, I sure will." The next day, Stewart came back with the completed papers. "Hi Mr. Rotchford, I've completely filled out the papers and I'm returning them to you," Stewart said. "Wonderful, I'm giving you a temporary building pass. Use this pass temporarily while your background investigation is ongoing and until you have clearance from the Secret Service to work at the White House." "I really thank you Mr. Rotchford," he said. "You're welcome, Stewart, and do your best!" Mr. Rotchford called out. "I promise that I will do my best!" Said Stewart, "You'll see." "I hope so, Stewart. We have another gentleman here by the name of Mr. Wilson who isn't doing a good job with the washing of the White House windows. Several people have complained about him. I don't want to go out on a limb for you and you disappoint the folks over there at the White House." "Oh no, I will do a great job. See I've been washing windows for years, so I have plenty of experience from working in our family-owned business that sort of fell through. But I want to thank you for this wonderful opportunity," said Stewart. Stewart began washing windows and the days were going by as fast as lighting strikes! It was about six months into it when Stewart felt he had run out of things to do. Stewart knew that he could make himself useful in another way. "Hello Mr. Scouten, I would like to meet with you," an optimistic Stewart said. "I've been washing windows for some time now, but there isn't enough work to keep me busy here. Is there any other work to do, maybe mirrors, chandeliers, candelabras, globe lights?" "Gee Stevens, I am rather surprised that you would run out of work with all these windows, how is it that you have nothing else to do?" "I work fast but produce quality results." "Well, let me walk around and inspect what you have cleaned," said Mr. Scouten. "Yeah the chandeliers are very dirty, if you can put your hands to work with these and get them sparkling it may work. Let me show you what you're working with," Scouten said, "These are very old chandeliers and they are some kind of dirty." "Yes but with my experience, I can make them look brand spanking new Mr. Scouten!" Stewart said. "I'm not trying to be rude, but they look like they have mud on them. Please give me a try." Stewart said. "Well okay. Hey fellas, get those scaffolds over there and put them all around. I have someone here that wants to prove himself with the chandeliers!" said Mr. Scouten. The painters put up scaffolds and Stewart began to clean the chandeliers in the cross hall. "Hey, man did you see that, those chandeliers have never looked like that before. That guy has a magic touch, looks like everyone is impressed!" "Hello what's all this fuss about?" asked one of the Housekeeping staff. "I'll tell you what the chatter is about; this new kid on the block has made the chandeliers look like a million bucks! He's good and he's fast, he's worked his way all around the White House and into the residential quarters. Mr. Stevens is busy, I saw him in one location trying to count all of the Chandeliers." "Hey what's up man, I'm trying to count the Chandeliers, but I have to get to the next one, so I guess I don't have time to count when I'm only hired to clean and polish them and wash windows. Whew! Makes my day go by pretty fast," said Stewart. "Soon it'll be time to go home to my wife and family," said Stewart. "Not so fast," someone in the back called out. "Hi Mr. Stevens, we got word that you are looking for more work. We will need some assistance in the carpenters shop and setup and breakdown of the podiums for various speakers." "Wow, word travels quickly around here," said Stewart! "That's because we are one big happy family. "At least for eight hours a day," one of the housekeeping staff said. "Sure, no problem!" said Stewart.

A gentleman from the Operations staff said, "If you are up for working any overtime, we could use some help in the evening at the State Dinner Events." "Oh not a problem, just tell me when and I'll make myself available." "Hi Mr. Stevens, my name is Mr. Allen, I'm the head Butler." "Pleased to make your acquaintance, Mr. Allen," said Stewart. "Welcome aboard!" "Thank you Mr. Allen, I'm glad to have arrived," said Stewart. "We are too, said the Butler. You won't be working directly with the butlers; I'll be seeing you every day and at some of the State Dinners Mr. Stevens." They eventually got to be very close friends.

One morning, the supervisor asked, "Stevens are you up to working a double today? We have a State event and many guests are coming which requires a few staff to work as coat checkers. Let me know if you are interested," said Mrs. Crans-Limerick. "Yes I am available," he said. The day had ended and he made a quick change from his informal uniform to formal attire. As the guests and celebrities were arriving, people were preoccupied and admiring the White House details and interior. One man said, "The chandeliers are just beautiful!" "Hello, may I take your evening coat?" said Stewart as he addressed a woman that had shimmering gold Austrian crystals lining the edge of her jacket. "Yes, thank you sir," she said. Stewart attended to the gentleman escorting the woman, "How about you sir, I'll take your coat and here is your ticket for pick up." While attending to a large group of other incoming guests, Stewart continuously took coats and provided a ticket for picking up. "Hey there, here comes Sammy Davis Jr. Oh this is just so exciting man," said a wide-eyed Stewart. "Yes it is, Stewart," said his colleague Matthew as he assisted with another incoming group of guests. "I sure wish that I could get to shake his hand or something, with the entertainers." "Aretha Franklin will be coming during one of the events next week." "Great, I've always liked Aretha Franklin; but I know I can't leave my post at the door to meet her," Stewart said. "Oh well, at least I got a glance and it sure is great seeing them in person, though! Wait until I tell my wife I saw Sylvester Stallone! That Stallone was dressed to kill and he wasn't pulling any punches! His tuxedo was awesome!"

FAMILY LIFE WHILE WORKING AT THE WHITE HOUSE

"Steve" (his name Steve was branded by White House staff) was not just a person who preferred to work his life away. He was husband first and dad, secondly.

At home, Calvin, was a fine family man and he found time outside of his busy schedule to have family cookouts, take some fishing, some to football practice, and some to basketball practice. Then there was a time he took one son during his teenage-years to what was called then, "The Capital Boulevard" and met several basketball stars. What fond memories of him and his youngest son. This was a fine time of togetherness and the two of them really enjoyed this time. This gave them a life-time of sharing and a loving father-son relationship.

At home, Stewart Calvin found time to take Marie to nice theatrical plays and movie flicks and out to eat. They loved the movies, (The Big Screens before Big Screen HD came to home theater). In particular, Calvin and Marie went to see the classics. He watched many of these same classics on DVD and Blue Ray in his later life; just reminiscing of times he shared with Marie.

Stewart Calvin, a die-hard (Commander) aka (Redskin in those days) fan . He did not miss a game! There was full of excitement and enthusiasm at the mention of a football game and especially the play-offs and Super Bowl during football season. After church (when he was able to be off on Sunday) he watched the games,

(Courtesy of Lynetta Stevens)

"Many of his co-workers would come over to our family home for entertainment or small get togethers. A few of them had small entrepreneur positions. For example, if we needed used cars as was the thing when we were younger, someone sold me a few used cars." "My favorite memories are of in October, 1977 upon getting married, my father brought home the most beautiful arrays of fall mums of all colors, and various names. (Chrysanthemums, Anemone Mums, Spoon Mums, Shasta Daisy Mums) to adorn our patio for my wedding reception. The White House horticulturist groundskeeper took a liking to him through vast demonstration! All of these memories are so fond and a demonstration of pure love... so much so that the patio was fully decorated. To top it off, he was so cool with swag in his black tuxedo walking me down the aisle. "I was so proud of him that day." As for Marie, "Mom made sure her daughter was really pretty and she helped me pick out my beautiful wedding gown making inspections as we went along, Mom adorning my hair and light make up artistry. This was my first time ever getting my hair Relaxed. Marie (Mom) always gave me an at-home Press & Curl in those days. I may not have been a "Girl Scout" or a "Brownie", but, for sure, I was her little girl that she made feel like a princess and now a grown up daughter. My Mom was very honored

and proud of me on the day of my wedding!" Marie planned the menu and designed the reception!

Calvin and Marie

Marie was an immaculate housekeeper and loathed any form of laziness! She earned her keep and some working as hard as she did. Like they say, "A woman's work is never done" and this held true for Marie. Each morning before Stewart left for work....you could hear Marie as she scurried from the bedroom to the kitchen to fix her husband's breakfast. She did this many years while he was working at the White House. She made sure he left home with a nice breakfast before start of day! Even when Stewart Calvin retired, she was still working. He did not cook, he did no laundry, he did no grocery shopping, he did no budgeting, decorating, no getting the children to school and all visits to dentist and hospital visits when anyone of them fell ill, it was Marie that got them to these appointments at times alone and at times with Calvin's help since he was the driver! A confidant and a friend to talk to, and share a cup of coffee with –that was Mom.

On another note, something of a hilarious moment, Marie was here to see to all business within the Stevens household while her husband was working. One day a Termite Inspector came to the home to check for termites. *The inspector went into one of the bedrooms as she sent him back to inspect. Marie was just around the corner and she noticed the inspector putting out termites from a small dispenser. "Well Ma'am , I sorry to tell you, but you all have termites". The termite inspector didn't realize she was standing right in behind him. She immediately came closer into the room, "Oh! No you don't! You get your bags and out of here right now! (Of course, it wasn't said that nicely).*

Marie is a sharp and quick person and you cannot get away with much. She does not miss a beat! I'm here to tell you.

(Courtesy of Lynetta Stevens)

As far as beauty goes, she still managed to get to hair appointments and shopping for herself and the children, that was Mom.

Stewart Calvin Stevens, was a good role model for his sons. He was a disciplinarian, yet it worked out for the good. All things considered…he did his best as husband and father! All that is required is that we do our Best, "Be The Best that You can Be". As time went by and they became grandparents, Stewart was known as the family Tooth Snagger" Yes, he had time to work at the White House and still pull teeth with sewing thread for his young grandchildren! The grandchildren as most children, wanted their teeth out in a hurry. Everyone wants the tooth fairy to come! Of course, not so much now (Laugh)

At the White House, Steve was well-respected. As recalled, "There were many times that he had friends skilled in various professions to assist with personal favors on their time for our family. As a favor to him, because he was well-liked, pictures were framed and wooden valances made by the White House carpenters to go over the living room windows in the early 70s".

I WAS WORKING AT the White House as The Chandelier Polisher and window washer, which consisted of cleaning all of the Chandeliers and the washing of all of the windows. Performing my job was less stressful because I had a very patient and understanding wife. I worked a double-shift during these days quite often. I was away from my family an average of 16 hours a day. I unrelentingly performed my duties as White House staff to the best of my abilities. But I always made it back home by nightfall. My wife would be waiting for me with a cup of tea, a bun, and a lot of love! And some nights Marie wanted me to listen to her read some of the writings of the book she had been writing called, *The Dawn of the Cameo Promise*, which was not published until 2013. My wife had written articles for the Washington Post during *Human Kindness Day* in 1975.

(Courtesy of Janice Marie Stevens)

(A Tribute to Marie…Mom you were a wonderful writer, author, and very intelligent. Your gift of writing was so inspirational and the manner in which you put it all together was as awesome as you Mom. You were ahead of your time. I love you MOM)

"BROADEN THE SCOPE OF HUMAN KINDNESS DAY"

Some people say there is no solution to the violence that occurred here on "Human Kindness Day" when you get a crowd of so many together. Others are saying we must find a solution, but it seems to be said with such an air of doubt.

I say that when we as human beings, can truly have a human kindness day in our hearts, as well as in our heads, the problem will most assuredly be solved.

When we can consider the cultural backgrounds of our sisters and brothers, we can truly have a beautiful "Human Kindness Day".

After all this world is not all black and white. Why not have a program pertaining to our many cultural backgrounds, such as gospel, country western, jazz, rock, opera and music from our golden era so our senior citizens can enjoy themselves as well as our young people.

If we had a program based on the interest of all people, then we could come together with appreciation, admiration, and respect for one another. This arrangement could also help control the number of people who would be present for any one program.

The United States presents many diverse people with many cultural backgrounds, each contributing something different from their own way of life and adopting some aspects of culture from a sister or brother from another culture.

Let us plan our programs to include our neighbors from the East and West, as well as our neighbors from the North and South of this great nation and come together as one Nation under God as we were taught as small children in our saluting of the Flag.

Janice M. Stevens- (See Faded News Article Attached)

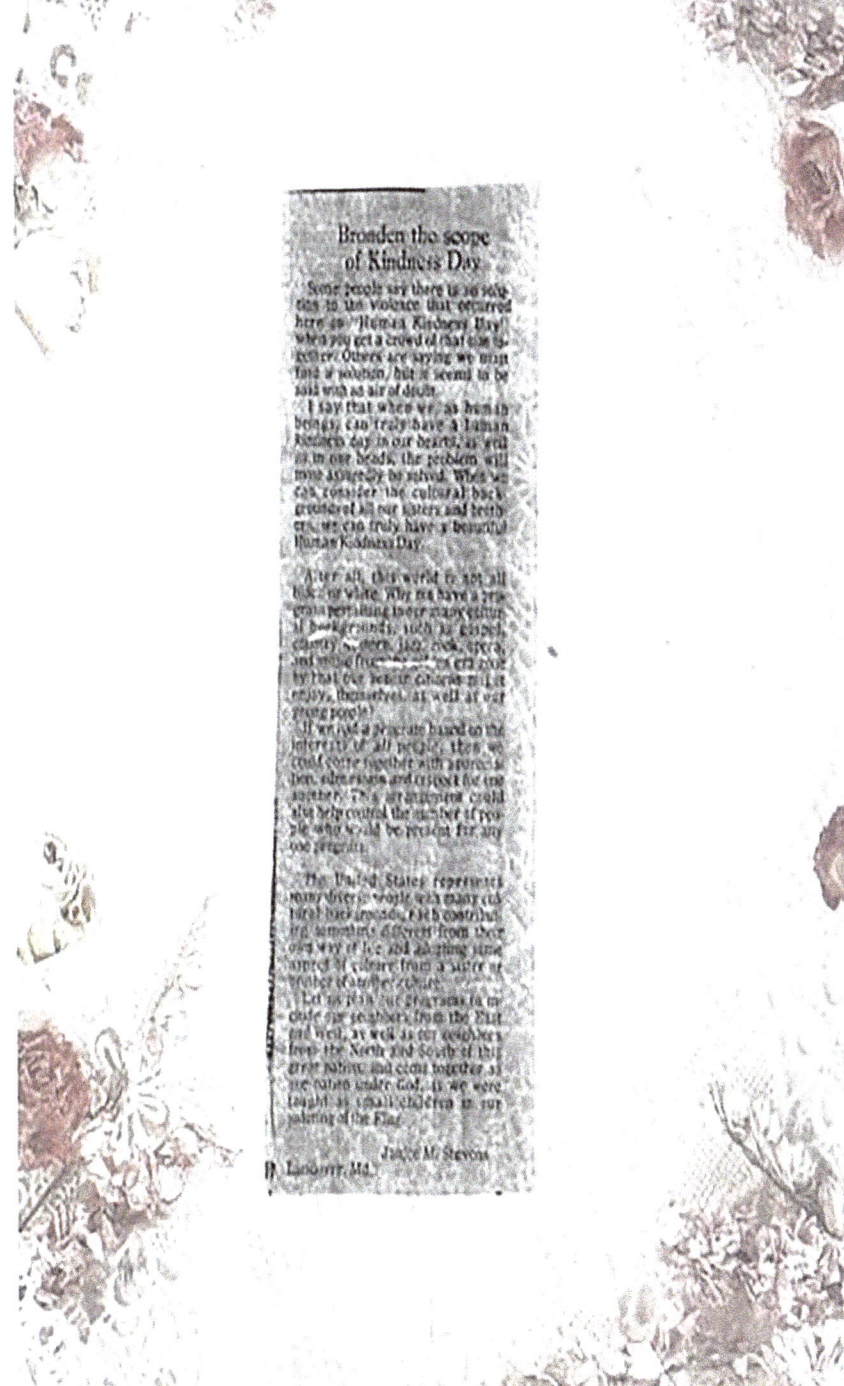

Broaden the scope of Kindness Day

Some people say there is no solution to the violence that occurred here on Human Kindness Day, when you get a crowd of that size together. Others are saying we must find a solution, but it seems to be said with an air of doubt.

I say that when we, as human beings, can truly have a human kindness day in our hearts, as well as in our heads, the problem will more assuredly be solved. When we can consider the cultural background of our sisters and brothers, we can truly have a beautiful Human Kindness Day.

After all, this world is not all black or white. Why not have a program prevailing in our many cultural backgrounds, such as gospel, country & western, jazz, rock, opera and what-have-you, so we can look by that our better citizens might enjoy themselves, as well as our young people?

If we had a program based in the interest of all people, then we could come together with a prosperous, calm vision and respect for one another. This arrangement could also help control the number of people who would be present for any one program.

The United States represents many diverse people, with many cultural backgrounds, each contributing something different from their own way of life and adopting some aspect of culture from a sister or brother of another culture.

Let us reach out our arms to include our neighbors from the East and West, as well as our neighbors from the North and South of this great nation and come together as one nation under God, as we were taught as small children in our saluting of the Flag.

Janice M. Stevens
Landover, Md.

On occasions I had to work during some of the White House events. However, during some events that I was not scheduled to work, I took my wife and my children to the South Lawn of the White House and watched the Independence Celebration and sometimes I carried them to the Easter Egg Roll. On the lighting of the National Christmas Tree, my family would watch it on television. They wanted me to take them to the lighting of the National Christmas Tree, but I generally had to work during most of these occasions and did not want them out in the cold. As the children got older, during summer months Marie enjoyed riding the Metro downtown to join me for lunch. From the beginning of my White House tenure up until the end, Marie was a loyal friend and cheerleader, cheering me on for the assignment set out before me.

Our family consisted of six children. While, I was working, my wife was home maintaining the household and caring for the children.

Our children were growing and thriving. Everybody on the job knew I was a family man because I was very private about my personal life and did not discuss my family business. There was nothing to say but the very best about my family.

On one occasion, my wife called down to the White House to the Ushers office to get me to call her back regarding a family matter.

They were unable to locate me. About an hour or so later I found out that the staff were looking for me. It was rather difficult to locate me if you did not know the exact area in which I was assigned to work. My wife left a message with the Ushers Office for me to call her because it was very important. She would never call for me unless it was very important because we were not in the habit of talking on the job. When I found out that she had called and I had not received the message, I got very angry and I went to the Ushers to find out why I never got the message, especially since we did not have this as a practice unless something was rather important. One of the doormen said he looked for me, but he didn't know where to find me. I told the Chief Usher, Mr. Rex Scouten, that if my wife ever calls again, please make sure that someone finds me immediately since she rarely calls. I called home and sure enough it was an emergency, one of my children needed medical attention and my wife needed me to meet her at the hospital.

When it came to my family I did not mess around, I left immediately and went to the hospital.

On the day the White House staff was paid, everyone received a salary check except me. As a result, I had to go to the Ushers Office again to find out why my check had not come and was told by the Chief Usher that apparently my supervisor had not put my time in and that I would have to wait until next pay to get my other check. This left me feeling very unhappy. I told the Ushers Office that someone was going to have to get me some money because I was the sole supporter of my family and lived from pay period to pay period. Therefore, I could not afford to wait for another two weeks to get my salary check. Mr. Rex Scouten then said, "Steve, don't worry, we will get you some money from Petty Cash that will hold you until we find out what happened to your check. I asked him how much money they would allow me to get from Petty Cash. He replied, "How would $100 be?" I told him that would not be sufficient enough to take care of my family for two weeks. He said, "I'll make arrangements to get you some money, Steve." I left out of the office and within an hour he called Jim Reilly, the supervisor of the Operations Office and he told him to drive me down to 1100 Ohio Drive where the Payroll Section was located and have them to cut me a check. They did cut me a check that had to be repaid out of my next salary check. That is when the word got out, "Don't mess with Steve's family or his money." I never had any more problems of them getting the message to me when my wife called or any problems concerning my salary being delayed.

This brings me to a very important point of how I got my name at the White House. My wife brought me a belt buckle that said "STEVE" made out of brass. I would shine my belt buckle each day before going to work and everyone knew me as Steve. I would wear my belt buckle coming from the East wing. When I would go down the steps to go into the Residence side, the Secret Service would say, "Hey Steve." In doing so I would push a button to get through the gate. All the Secret Service would say, "Steve, let me see that belt buckle so we know it's you," and everyone would laugh. I would show my belt buckle and Federal ID pass to get through the gate. I was then well known as "Steve," short for Stevens, and that is what they called me.

(Courtesy of Stewart C. Stevens)

The White House had seven different teams on the bowling league, and at time the guys didn't know there was a team by the name of the Happy Hookers. I had bowled for about three weeks before we knew there was a women's team by the name of the Happy Hookers. I started to participate in this league but when my wife found out that the name of one of the teams was *The Happy Hookers*, that ended my bowling career and I did not bowl on that league any longer!

My wife, Marie, enjoyed me talking about the entertainers that came to the White House and other small talk. She was well aware that we did not discuss anything of what went on at the White House. I told her in the beginning of my career that anything that happens in the White House stays in White House. My wife protected and instructed everyone, including the children, that our phones were not for talk about anything concerning the White House. She was definitely the First Lady of our house!

"Morning, sweetheart how are you," said Marie. "Well you start your new job at the White House today. I am so excited for you Calvin," she said. "Thanks, honey. I appreciate you giving me this wonderful breakfast." "Yes dear, you're welcome. I have a wonderful lunch all packed for you, she said." As Calvin sat there just beaming at how wonderful his life was and happy that he could finally provide financial security for his family, he began to thank God. The rain came pouring as he sat there enjoying a bite before the children awoke. "Hi Daddy," said his son. "Hello, how's my son this morning?" "I'm fine Dad. I woke up excited because the teacher in my history class was talking a lot about the government places that are important like the US Capitol, the White House, and the National Monument and all. The fourth graders are planning on taking a school trip downtown to the city part of Washington DC. I am so proud that my dad will be working at the White House where all of the Presidents live." "Me too, I am so proud of you Daddy," a little voice came from behind the bedroom door. A starry-eyed little boy with a high-pitched voice said, "me too daddy, I'm so proud of you." "What's all this chatter? You boys are up so early this morning," Calvin said. Normally the children weren't up so early. "Thank you boys," their Dad said. "Listen up; your Daddy wants all of you to do well in school. Keep your grades up so that you all will have nice professions when you are all grown up and on your own." "Well, honey, I had better be going." "Yes dear, I'll be thinking of you on this big day," Marie said. "Honey if you can call me today in between your breaks or something, I'll be right by the phone waiting just to hear your voice say hello. We can talk later today when I see you," she said. "I know you will be pretty busy." "Baby, I wouldn't let the day go by without calling to tell you how much I love you! It'll be brief, though. Everyone have a nice day" "You too, Daddy!" they all shouted. Calvin grabbed his wife and kissed her as he picked up his umbrella and lunch box and headed out the door.

"Good evening! Well, how was it"? Marie said. "Oh, I like the position that I have. The staff were all so nice and I had the chance to meet the Chief of the Staff to whom I am assigned. I briefly saw President Richard Nixon. He's a nice person. My job is not only restricted to washing windows and cleaning chandeliers. My duties will also include working some nights at State dinners and events. I may have to work a double tomorrow," Calvin said. "Honey, I hope you can handle the fact that I may have more days like that," Calvin said. "Oh, sure, whatever you have to do to get the job down. I am just so happy for you, and so happy for us!" she said. "This is a wonderful opportunity. It's not every day that a Black man can work at the President's house. I know they are going to be pleased with my hardworking husband. Besides, the children will keep me busy for that time you are working. Calvin, did I tell you that I am writing articles to the Washington Post and I have a book that I am writing which will take some time. It will be titled *The Dawn of the Cameo Promise.* "Oh, that is wonderful honey. I look forward to reading it all one of these days," Calvin said. "Well, honey, if you aren't too tired, can you read some of my story now"? "Sure honey," she said. "Hi daddy, how are you?" "How's my girl today?" asked her dad. "I'm doing great and all, working hard in school you know, and helping Mama out with chores in the evening. Mama gives me a break, though, so I can focus on my homework assignments." "Yeah, your Mom is swell, isn't she?" "Yes, Mom is swell Dad, she's a good mother to us children, and smart too!" "Well, what's for dinner? I'm starved because I am burning more energy," Calvin said. "Honey dinner is ready and waiting. Children hurry and eat, do your homework, and settle down for bed. I have some special dessert made just for your Dad!" Marie said. "Yes Ma'am" they all sang out in chorus.

Later that evening, "Good Night children, we'll see you all in the morning. Where's the little baby boy?" "He's alright daddy. We all take turns getting him off to sleep."

"Where's the dessert sweetheart?" asked Calvin. "Baby I got it served up. As the appetizer you will be served a cup of tea, a nice cinnamon pecan bun, and coming right up is a Whole Lot of Love!" "Sounds good to me baby!" he said. "Sounds mighty, mighty good!" he said. "I'll put a sign on the door of the kitchen saying *Kitchen Closed*," she said, and the lights went out.

"Good morning, kids. I have special invitations as White House staff to take everyone to see the fireworks on the South Lawn of the White House. Is anyone interested?" said Calvin. "Yay, yay, we get to go to the White House for the Fourth of July!" "Honey, that is really nice," Marie said. "Yes sweetheart, it is thoughtful of them to give us a special invitation." "Daddy, we're all ready to go down and see the fireworks on the South Lawn of the White House!" "I would also like to go to the White House for the Easter Egg Roll although that's not until next year," Marie said. "That was already in the back of my mind. I remember how last Easter turned out when we had our own little Easter Egg Roll at the house," said Calvin. "Last year during our little Easter egg fiasco, I wanted to hide it somewhere in the house but since you are so good at finding things, I had to eat it because I wasn't sure where to hide it, Baby. I panicked when I could not decide where to hide it and quickly ate it. Let me assure you that this will never happen again, because we are going to the Presidential Easter Egg Roll and that is safer." "Okay, Calvin, No more sneaky attacks, promise?" "Alright baby, I don't want to risk our love loss due to an Easter egg!" Calvin said. They looked at one another and smiled as the children broke out in laughter.

(Courtesy of WH Photographer)

Some years passed by and corporate America has started this event called *Bring Your Children to Work Day*. Calvin, speaking calmly to his wife, said, "Honey since our three older children have other school obligations and they cannot get away, I thought it would be a great idea to take the smaller ones. I sure wish they had this when the others were younger at school," the other one said with excitement. Like Mama always said, "You are to call them Associates." One of her famous lines was "You don't have any friends on the job or in school, you only have associates."

"Calvin, I have a surprise for your birthday!" "What is it honey? "I brought you a nice belt buckle, and it says **STEVE**. It is brass and if you keep it shined up they'll all know who you are," Marie said. "Put it on and let me see you wear it in style," she laughed out loud. "Aww honey, that is so sweet of you," he said. As Calvin put it on he said, "This is wonderful. I like the brass –it feels so rich and shines so bright. Girl, this makes me feel some kind of special!" "You are special, you're my man and I couldn't resist it when I saw it, baby."

"Hey Steve, like that belt buckle, man," said one of his colleagues at the White House. "Oh yeah, my wife bought it for me and she paid a fine penny for it." "Wow, she wants everyone to know who her man is," the colleague said. "Yeah, man, she loves me like that, you dig? You know I'm a lucky man," Stewart blushingly said. As the days went by, even people that worked in various departments of the White House came to know him as Steve. The Presidents came to know him on a more personal level. It was a blustery windy morning in March after his birthday while staff members were going into the White House, and he had the belt on. "Hello, please show us your ID badge and we'll buzz you through, alright thank you. Next!" said the Secret Service, while quickly getting the staff through during the morning rush. "Next! Please place your personal belongings on the security machine. Next! Please swipe your Federal ID Badge sir, and we'll buzz you in," said the Secret Service.

"Let me see your badge. Oh, we got it, Stevens. Hey, we like your belt buckle, it looks real rich," the Secret Service said. "What does it say?" "It says STEVE, short for Stevens," Stewart said. "We like that. Ok just swipe your badge and come on through."

"Good morning, STEVE! Welcome to the East Wing. Now let me see that buckle so we all can make sure it's you, show your badge and we'll buzz you on through. Have a good day!" "Thank you Sir," Steve replied.

In fact, that strong belief of how Calvin came into the position was of a force unbeknownst to him.

Now as far as caring for the family, Marie provided the spiritual aspects for the family and this was a practical thing within her family of origin. Yet, Calvin was a man of faith! And this is what it took for him each day on his journey to the U.S. White House getting up and out! Although Calvin worked a lot on weekends, he attended church service when he could. The White House had work on Sunday shifts. When needing spiritual guidance, they sought together. She gave Calvin his personal Bible in the late 70s. Special moments like these were very memorable.

Through the working of tedious projects day in and day out, you can't break one crystal, you can't break any windows, and you can't slip on a window ledge or break your back and Oh! I have to balance my weight so as not to take a fall!! And Oh, I'm the only one doing this job for the entire Estate! My goodness, what a tedious job that required so much concentration and discipline!! Yes! "Steve" needed faith and so much guidance just for getting up there in the distance every day to clean 147 windows at 1600 Pennsylvania Avenue NW. The Chandeliers alone were heavy in weight and in high altitude.

(Courtesy of Lynetta Stevens)

Calvin always wanted to be a police since he was a Military Police (MP) in Germany; yet that was a dream that never became a reality. He was not destined to become a Metropolitan DC police for whatever reason. And second, Marie never wanted her husband to be a police. She often would say, "Honey this would be such a stressful job. What would I do if something happens to you?" She was ahead of her time and capable of seeing how crime would be on the rise. Times were definitely changing and more so now during this era.

His faith is what got him to the White House and His faith in the Almighty is who and what kept him!!

When Stewart Calvin was able to attend church; he did it in style. Since he had to wear the grey or Khaki material uniform which was practical for the work of the White House staff; he wasn't able to dress in style. So when possible, he liked to dress up in his sharp suits which gave him that extra ego boost and swag, even as a seasonably mature gentleman.

MY FAITH, kept me from fear of climbing an approximately 30-foot scaffold in order to clean the three largest chandeliers in the White House. Each one had over 6,000 pieces of Bohemian cut glass and I could not break any of them – and I did not in over 34 years. And one other thing that really kept me motivated was Dr. Martin Luther King's speech: "What I'm saying to you this morning, my friends, even if it falls your lot to be a street sweeper, go on out and sweep streets like Michelangelo painted pictures; sweep streets like Handel and Beethoven composed music; sweep streets like Shakespeare wrote poetry; sweep streets so well that all the host of heaven and earth will have to pause and say, 'Here lived a great street sweeper who swept his job well.'"

These quotes I applied to my position during my years at the White House as the Chandelier Polisher Specialist and Polisher and window washer. I thought to myself daily, "If it falls my lot to be a Chandelier Polisher and a window washer, polish chandeliers and wash windows so that all the hosts of heaven and earth will pause and say here lives a great Chandelier Polisher. Be the best at whatever you do."

Regarding the assassination of Dr. Martin Luther King, it was a sad time in history. During the rioting and looting in Washington DC, my brother and I were riding through the city trying to get to our window washing jobs. As we were coming from one of our jobs, coming down H Street, NE, and we were approached by a couple of guys carrying an arm full of suits. We were conscious- minded and did not steal. This is one of the reasons that my record remained clean. We had values of integrity and were taught not to steal or accept stolen goods from any one, which reminds me of another incident that demonstrates my sense of integrity.

The incident that I am referring to is involving the United States Treasury Department during the Nixon administration when on February 21, 1974 I walked from the White House over to the Treasury Department to go cash my salary check. While walking through the Treasury corridors, I noticed a check with documents attached. The documents were facing upward. I picked them up and looked at them. I could not believe my eyes when I saw the amount of the check. The fact that someone would lose a check with such a great sum of money was mind-boggling. On the paper there were instructions typed in to say, "Deliver to Room 204." I proceeded to go down the hall to that office. When I opened the door and went in, the Secretary approached me and asked if she could help me. I told her Yes Ma'am. I explained to her that I had just found this in the hallway and it had to be delivered to Room number 204. When she looked at the check she went to get her supervisor. She looked stunned and came back out with her manager. The manager then said, "May I help you Sir"? I said, "Yes Sir my name is Stewart Stevens and I work over at the White House." I told him that I found this check with all of these documents attached and it is supposed to be delivered here so I brought it down to deliver it to you guys. He then said, "Are you sure you work at the White House?" and asked me for my full name and my supervisor's name. He thanked me very much; I turned around and went back into the White House. After getting back to work at the White House, I saw my supervisor, Mr. Scouten, the Chief Usher and I told him about the incident of me finding the check in the amount of $14,500,000 (fourteen-and-a-half *million*) with the necessary documents attached. Mr. Scouten, then said, "Steve you did the right thing," and I continued on to do my job.

About two weeks later Mr. Scouten called me into his office and told me that the Treasury Department sent me an award of $50. Most people in my position would have avoided this situation. As White House staff, I found this predicament to be rather awkward. Most people would have avoided the situation entirely, because getting involved placed me in a vulnerable position as the matter did not directly concern me. I was not a Treasury employee, but White House Staff passing through the Treasury Department to handle personal business on my lunch hour. And for this kind gesture, I was rewarded a menial monetary award of $50 (which turned into a measly $40 after taxes were taken out). I did not wish to mention it to any President for fear of jeopardizing my career, but it seems it should have been more.

As I look back over the 42 years from February 1974 to February 2016, I wonder if I had not been a White House employee, how much finder's fee I would have received. I am still patiently waiting for the Treasury Department to make a decision on how much finder's fee they feel I am entitled to. Yet I had faith that if you do the right thing, things always work.

Glossy marble floors, glowing from the sun in the arched windows caused Steve to look down and take notice of some confidential documents and a check for $14.5 million in the Treasury corridor. "Whoa, what a check," Steve said. "Let me hurry and turn this check in –it's hot! There ain't no way in the world someone could lose a check this big!" he thought to himself while walking down the Treasury corridor.

"Hi Mr. Scouten, how are you today?" said Steve. "Fine and how are you Steve"? "Well I stumbled across a check as I was going down the corridors in the Treasury Building and I realize I had to turn it in. I could have passed over it and kept going, but since it had a stack of important documents related to the close-out of a federal project, I picked up the package. I know that without these documents and the check, the transaction would not be completed," said Steve. "Mr. Scouten, I knew these had to be turned in right away. I'm sure that someone had timelines to complete and I just wanted to make sure that the check was in the right hands. I felt it was the right thing to do." "You're so right Steve, you did the right thing, and I'm proud of you. As a matter of fact, I am going to speak the Treasury Department officials and see what they can do about giving you an award for being honest and acting in a timely manner. It would have been an inconvenience for them." Mr. Scouten said. "Yes it would have; I really thank you Sir," Steve said.

That evening, Steve shared with his wife about the incident. "Honey, guess what happened to me today? I found a check; a large check with some documents attached while over in the Treasury Department." "What! How much was it for?" "Honey, it was $14.5 *million* dollars." "Really?" Marie said. "Well Baby, you did the right thing by turning the check and documents in; I'm proud of you for that. I sure hope they give you a nice reward, at least a one percent finder's fee." "Yeah, that would be nice," Calvin said. "Well let's call it a day. The Lord will bless you. Hopefully, they will give you a good reward for finding it. Things will work out better in the long run.

"Another day, another day," Calvin said as he awoke to get ready for work. He drove off, headed towards work and pulled into his assigned parking space. "Hey there Steve, Good morning," said his co-workers. "Hey fellows, do you know what happened to me yesterday? Well, I was walking over to the Treasury Department to cash my salary check, and while walking I found this check for $14.5 million dollars," said Steve. "Aww Steve, stop lying. You ain't found no check for $14.5 million dollars." "Just wait awhile and you'll hear about it."

(Courtesy of Stewart C. Stevens Sr.)

As the sun broke through the clouds on a day that appeared to be a rather calm one, Calvin made a call to his mother. "Hi Mom, how are you and Dad doing? I've been working so hard and all. Trying to catch my breath between work and home and been meaning to drop by to see you all."

"Yes son," she said. "We sure miss you too." "Everyone's doing good and the family will be up to visit real soon," said Calvin. "Say Mom, I've been thinking of old times with you and how we used to sit and talk for a while." "I'm so glad to hear from you son," she said. "Listen, would you like to have a little tea party with me for old time's sake?" She said.

"Why of course Mom, I will be up in a few days to have that cup of tea and cookies like we used to do when I was a child. Only this time, I have a nice picture with me and one of the Presidents. One of the carpenters down here framed it for you." "Oh great!" I will place that right on my wall over the dining room table. I'll see you next week and look forward to our tea time once again!" "Mama, I have something to tell you concerning a large check that I found and turned in." "Oh my, did you get a reward or any recognition?" she said. "A small one, nothing to brag about," he said. "But it was nice just holding it and looking at for a while." "Okay, we'll talk when I see you son, Love you." "Tell Dad I said hello," he said, "and I love you too Mama."

PART III

THE CHANDELIER HISTORY FACTS and LIFE

A GLIMPSE FROM THE TOP: THE HISTORY OF THE CHANDELIERS

As reported to us (Stewart and me) both, during an interview with the White House Historical Association in 2019, and quoted, "The White House Chandeliers were cleaned and polished differently up until the Eisenhower Administration. They were taken from the vaulted ceilings as lifted on chains and cleaned with soap and water and dried with paper towels. In those days, no one went up there on a scaffold. Once the Chandelier was pulled down on the floor, it took four to five White House housekeeping staff, to clean and polish the chandeliers" (As quoted by, Staff of the White House Historical Association, Washington, DC, 2019) "Steve" as they called him, was the only one that went up to these 30 ft. high gigantic Chandeliers!

THE WHITE HOUSE
HISTORICAL ASSOCIATION

IT IS WHAT IT IS, A "GLIMPSE" FROM THE TOP, The White House Chandeliers are a piece of furnishing just as any other piece of furnishing. Chandeliers, light globes, candelabras, wall sconces are all lighting in various homes, building, for example, the U.S. Capitol, The Senate Office Buildings. In this instance, we are speaking of the "White

House" Chandeliers". Although it would be remiss not to mention that Stewart C. Stevens, Sr. cleaned everything that was glass in the White House. (I must say this, at times in the federal government we are told to perform other duties or "Other duties as Assigned" is listed within the Position Description and we are therefore, voluntold. If you are a federal employee, this is a given as I can attest). When voluntold on a day, it's something we never signed up for such as in the Heidelberg, Germany incident. One day they asked Stewart (Not "Steve" ....he didn't have the Belt Buckle yet! Laugh) to work kitchen duty to fill in for one day. They were short on staff. He did this without any hesitation. Although this was not his duty of hire nor was it something he would be proud of; simultaneously, it's nothing to be ashamed of since you knew the big picture. He never minded helping though. May this be a lesson to this generation...."Other duties as assigned" especially during a crisis.

(Courtesy of Lynetta Stevens)

Now let's circle back to "The Chandeliers" please. Emphasis is mostly put on the Chandeliers, because they are the most delicate, intricately designed, and biggest of all! I've examined a large chandelier for myself prior to making a purchase for *The Play*, "The White House Chandeliers" held in July 2019, Washington, DC. *The crystals to the Chandeliers are intertwined in brass or bronze grooves and intricate parts that require sometimes dismantling of or actually going into the deep and special parts. This is necessary just to get to the dust and ensure that the dirt is removed. It's definitely a unique process and especially so when one would have to go up in the height (A Glimpse at the Top) of where they hung. This took a special person do this specialized work and have them shining so brightly.*

For example, one could have a sporty vehicle, say a Mercedes, if the vehicle is dirty and run down, so to speak…just like anything else, the focus of attention is not prevalent. It's a tangible item and without waxing, polishing, upkeep or maintenance, well it's nice; however, no one really puts a focus on it. Therefore, no one says, like ooh! awe! On the other hand, if it's clean, polished, and driven around, often heads turn. People say Wow! What a nice ride that is! "Man that is gorgeous!" and someone might say, "Who's driving this baby?", "It is clean!! Or "She's a beauty!"

When tourists came to the White House, (Back in the day, there used to be so many tourists coming to the White House) they looked in awe at everything and all the furnishings. On occasion, the Chandeliers were a topic of discussion. Steve was able to wave from a distance to the visitors. The admiration of how beautiful they looked was not important to me. But as for me, the one that wondered how my father did this job, it was an amazement and an admiration for the man that polished them and not for the Chandeliers, a tangible thing. Often you wonder when people look at things do they ever think of the person behind the luxurious! Steve did them so well and he was proud of his workmanship. He was proud that he never ever broke "One" nor did he break one piece of crystal. He was happy that others were getting enjoyment of the Chandeliers beauty and the rays of sparkle that they reflected onto the rugs. It's as if gifts are bestowed upon us. Yet oftentimes we are reflecting more on the tangible, rather than the one that provides the tangible for us to enjoy. Yes! Steve was gifted to us and he poured himself out.….it was more than a career for him and it was how he was with his wife and children.

An "instrument" that was not cross-trained and which had no back-up person to do this job. An "instrument" that worked like a machine as one man by himself. "He was the reason the Chandeliers beamed" as quoted, *in the song. "One Man, His Faith, and His Love" copyright 2019, written expressly for The Play. There, in the White House, were many butlers, maids, others of profession, yet one Stewart Calvin Stevens, that did ALL these Chandeliers! And ALL lighting and ALL Windows (147) with Entrance Doors, and Working the State Dinners when possible for overtime. Juggling like Steve did was commendable and he did it for his family! What was good, Steve got a little chance to enjoy, the camaraderie of social life during the dinners and small talk with various Presidents. He enjoyed, his career and that was amazing!*

*Let's understand, Steve was not worked as a slave nor was he a 'YES' man. This was a privilege to work in the U.S. White House as staff; yet still he earned benefits as a federal employee to provide for his family. Stewart expresses this in one of his chapters, "Don't mess with his family and "Don't mess with his money". Stewart kept his earn by working! Simply working! No Okedoke! No servitude! He gave respect and they respected him in return. Work was not all serious....*there were some humorous and fun times!

(Courtesy of White House Photographer)

CHANDELIER ELEGANCE

The Chandeliers were elegant! As, you stated several times, The Chandeliers were dirty before you came. You stated and I quote, "I had nothing else to do after the windows and I requested to clean one after I did the windows."

Stewart Calvin "Steve"--they were "elegant"! You made them elegant! The gift of creativity was bequeathed to YOU in the master plan. That is my inheritance too. Inheritance comes not only through monetary... inheritance is talents, gifts, moments cherished, and thankfully, so. How rich we are because of gifts... craftsmanship, intellect; intuition, determination, and faith (The ability to grab a hold of nothing until it becomes something is immensely divine)! "I don't see it, yet I believe it". "I don't have to see it to believe it ....I believe it prior to seeing it". Thanks for bequeathing this same foresight that you both had.

Stewart Calvin, you could see the crystals sparkling before you even went up to clean and polish "The Chandeliers". That's Elegance!

(Courtesy of White House Historical Association)

MY STORY IS FEATURED in the book published in 1975 called *The Working White House*, which was written by Haynes Johnson and photographed by Frank Johnson and was published by Praeger Publications. This book is still in print and can be purchased from online bookstores. This book was given to all the White House staff employees. My photograph is on page nine. There is one picture of me in the Preface as the book began and also on the back of the cover when the book ends. Then, starting on page 63 is when the authors include details of my job alongside my picture, and on page 64 is where my colleague talks about the work that I continued to do at the White House. There is an article featured in *The Working White House*: "And always in the background at the White House are the ubiquitous workmen performing their daily and endless maintenance task, one man works full time to wash all the windows. 'We will never find another person like that again,' remarked one White House employee, 'He's got his job down to a science. When he finishes with the windows, he then washes and polishes all the Chandeliers. However, The Chandeliers became my first priority. Other White House Aids pay no attention as he stands on a ladder in the vaulted arched hallway on the ground floor out of site of the public tourists.'" Also featured on the National Geographic DVD, *Inside the White House*, narrated by Morgan Freeman is Steve, climbing the ladders and cleaning the foyer.

My job was tedious and dangerous. For example, one picture shows me cleaning outside of the North entrance while I was up in the air on the ladder. There was a glass enclosure directly under me and if I had fallen it would have been a fatality.

(Courtesy of Ronald Regan Presidential Library)

(Courtesy of Washington Post)   (Courtesy of White House Photographers)

I really liked polishing the Chandeliers because I worked by myself. Nobody had to supervise me because they knew I would do my work, and this was stated by Mrs. Crans-Limerick in my performance evaluation, and I quote "Steve does not need any supervision; he does his work." Mrs. Crans-Limerick was a superb Housekeeper. She was head of the Housekeeper union and an excellent supervisor. It was no secret to her who was working and who was goofing off. Each morning when Mrs. Crans-Limerick arrived she would come to the East Room. I would be on the scaffold working and she would say, "Hi, how are you doing Steve?" "Fine," I would reply. There were three antique light globes down the arched hallway. Each Monday, I would take them down, clean them and polish and shine them all.

Mrs. Crans-Limerick had an Assistant that needed to know everybody's job so that if the designated person was not there to do the job, the Assistant would be able to serve in the capacity of back-up. As a result, the houseman had to show the Assistant Housekeeper their job as a form of cross training. The houseman came and told me that the Assistant Housekeeper wanted to see me. He called me into his office to speak with me about showing him how to do my job. I told him that I wasn't going to show him my job because he wouldn't be able to do it anyway. The Assistant went to the Usher's Office and told the Chief Usher that I refused to show him my job. At that point, the Usher called me to the office and said to me, "Steve everybody here has to show the Assistant Housekeeper their job so that if you are not here the job can be done." The next day, the Assistant Housekeeper wanted to go with me upstairs onto the second floor so I could show him how to do my job. I then showed him how to get out of the window correctly with the safety belt so he wouldn't fall and have an injury. I got out of the window and showed him how to hook the safety belt while getting out of the window. I provided the procedures to him on how the job was to be done proficiently so he would not fall. One of the procedures is once you get out of the window, you have to lean back as far as you can because once you are out there it seems almost like you are hanging in thin air. We went through this procedure and he was unable to perform the task or master my job as the window washer.

Just today as I am writing my story as The Chandelier Polisher and window washer of the White House, I recently had a brief encounter with an old associate that works down at the White House. He is still a White House employee and I am not at liberty to disclose his identity. He and I started reminiscing about old times.

I would like to quote Dr. Martin Luther King: "Be a bush if you can't be a tree. If you can't be a highway, just be a trail. If you can't be the sun, be a star. For it isn't by size that you win or fail. Be the best of whatever you are." And now I know that my Heavenly Father has blessed me to do this work as good as I have done it and I know that I am the Best at what I do!

"Evening, evening everyone," Calvin said. He stumbled into the house as if he was a child excited about a new toy. The atmosphere was so homey and it smelled as if you had just walked into the corner bakery. "Hey what's that smelling so good? "Baby, I just got through baking a cake," Marie said. "Well that's great," said Calvin. "Honey we got some kind of a connection, you and I. How did you know that I am featured on several pages in this book *The Working White House* and they have nothing but good things to say about me?" "That's wonderful news," she said. "Let's show the children, they'll be delighted."

"Hi Daddy, I like the book. They said that you have your work down to a science! I like that dad." "Yeah, that sure is the truth," said Calvin. "It's as if you know how to keep going throughout the day, you don't stop. You finish with one project and go on to the next washing and polishing of The Chandeliers. "Wow! You impress me to want to be something like you when I grow up." "Why thank you, son. I didn't have much of an education, but you will do better with an education." "Yes Dad. One thing I admire about you is your work ethic. That's truly awesome. Education alone doesn't give you that, you either have it or you don't." "Did you know you are also featured on the National Geographic DVD narrated by Morgan Freeman? "Really?" Stewart said. "Yes Sir, You really are." "Okay, we'll all sit down and watch together first chance we get." "Cool! Sounds like a great idea," said his son.

On the next morning the Housekeeper greeted Mr. Stevens, "Good morning, Steve," said Mrs. Crans-Limerick as she gleefully walked out into the East Room. "My, my, Steve, you sure do a wonderful job with these chandeliers. You're so energetic and really a go-getter; catching all the dust and all from the Chandeliers!"

"Why thank you Mrs. Crans-Limerick," said Steve. "I like doing my job. You know these crystals are a reflection of the place but also a reflection of me. It's nothing like doing a half job. I truly appreciate you too as my Supervisor. With your high-spirited management style and providing such great incentives you give me the fuel to keep the engine going." Steve walked around and looked at the chandeliers and windows, admiring the work as he completed each task.

In the afternoon a crowd of tourists came and gathered around as they passed through each room of the White House. The tour guide led the way with such crowds as they beheld the décor of each room. As Steve was on the scaffold in the East Room, the crowd waved and Steve gave a bashful smile to the crowd of tourists. "Hey up there," they called. "Hello," he said with a larger smile, grinning from ear to ear. One of the guides said, "That is Mr. Stevens, The Chandelier Polisher, see how nicely they sparkle!".

"Steve, there will be a gala with dancing and all in the lobby tomorrow evening. Please see if you can assist the Operations staff with the moving of the Steinway Piano." "Of course I will," he said. After that Steve returned to the North Portico to clean the main arched window.

Stewart C. Stevens while waiving to the crowd below.

(Courtesy of White House Photographers)

The Chandeliers and windows had always been the main job for Stewart Stevens, although he had several other duties and completed various assignments. "Hi folks," Steve said, "How are you all doing today?" he said while standing outside on stretcher with a pail of water, wiper and rag. "Boy do those windows shine! I can see the reflection of the glass. It's so crystal clear I felt as if I could walk right through the glass, Steve!" "Your magic hands are at work again, the man with the magic hands!" He laughed, "Man go head, I'd like to see you try walking through the glass," he said jokingly with one of the housekeeping staff. "I'll put in a good word to Mrs. Crans-Limerick for you, Steve." "Alright man, that's awfully kind of you," said Steve.

"Hi, Mrs. Crans-Limerick. The Chandeliers, windows, globes and all are really beaming. I tell you I don't know how we did it before he came to work here. All of the lighting was so dingy and dirty, you remember don't you Mrs. Crans-Limerick?" "Yes, I sure do," said Mrs. Crans-Limerick. "He has truly made a difference." "Who cleaned the chandeliers and windows before anyway?" asked the staff worker. "I believe it was someone named, uh…," "I don't know, I'll have to check. But since I've been assigned to this staff as the housekeeper there has been nothing but praise and shouts out to you Steve. I've definitely noticed the amount of work he puts out and the quality of the work as well." "Thank you for the recommendation, I'll see to it that he is rewarded for his extra-mile attitude. He goes over and beyond the call of duty and makes it easier for the guests; he speaks and is friendly to everyone! I sure would hate to lose him to the State Department. I had word that he went on an interview with the State Department, but we hate to see him go," said Mrs. Crans-Limerick. "In fact, right this very moment I'm going to contact our Personnel Department and start the process," she said. "I decided not to leave Mrs. Crans-Limerick," said Steve. "Thank you for changing the series and the title of my position to that of a more professional one!"

Within a few months, management of the Housekeeping had made a decision to cross-train staff to provide back-up support for others when out of the office on vacation or leave. As a result, an Assistant Housekeeper was appointed to Mrs. Crans-Limerick.

"Hello, Mr. Stevens, I am assigned to support you in your duties as The Chandelier Polisher and window washer here at the White House. It has been told to me that you are to train me on your duties and techniques of washing the windows and cleaning and polishing the Chandeliers," he said. "Oh, you think you can handle it, huh? Well let's get started," said Steve. "First you must watch me while I demonstrate. I'm going to lead by example, so you will have to pay close attention," Steve said. "We can get started tomorrow if that's alright." "Sure I'm ready bright and early tomorrow morning," the Assistant Housekeeper replied.

First thing the next morning, "Hey Steve, I'm ready to get started with the window washing demonstration." "Alright, let's go," said Steve. "Uh…Uh… getting up these steps is a job in and of itself!" said the Assistant. "Man, we're just getting started, are you tired just from climbing the stairs to get to the upper levels?" "Yeah…but I'll make it because I really want to learn and master this job," he said as beads of sweat formed on his forehead. "Well let's catch the elevator. Okay, we're here. I'm going to put this stretch band on." "Hey what's this for?" "Well, you have to put it around your waist. Are you still watching me?" "Yes, Steve, I'm watching." "Good," said Steve. The day was clear but a little brisk. "Whew man, it's a little brisk but I'm back in now. Here you go, your turn," Steve said. What Steve observed was someone that looked as if they were shaking in their boots and sweat rolling down his fear-filled face. "Now, you have to put the safety belt on and get out there just like I showed you. Just keep a clear mind about it, man, and think positive and it'll be alright." As he took the safety belt, Steve touched his cold clammy hand and could tell that he was nervous and afraid. "I sure hope you're able to handle this, my friend," said Steve. It took some effort to get out of the window as he hesitantly took his foot off and on the ladder, several times. "Well, I'm out here, whew, I'm starting to feel dizzy up here." With eyes so wide as if they were bulging out of his head, the Assistant was in fear of his life. "Steve! Steve! Where are you? Steve! Steve you got to be crazy to get out there like that and hang out on a safety belt."

In the back of his mind Steve started thinking once he saw what was happening. He heard his wife's voice in the back of his mind as she had reminded him the night before as she consoled him, "Calvin, just go ahead and show him your job, I have a gut feeling he is not going to be able to do it" and he felt a calmness. "Man, stop shaking like that or you'll give us both a heart attack. I'm right here," said Steve. "Steve, I can't do that," he said. "You said you wanted to do my job, so this is what you have to do. We are going to have to go downstairs and talk to the Usher and I want you to tell him just what you just said. When we get to the Ushers Office, I want you to tell the Chief Usher what you told me upstairs," said Steve. "Hi Chief, I'm sorry to have to tell you this, but I can't do Steve's job and I can't go up high. "Why didn't you tell me that?" asked the Usher. "You seemed so confidently assured and coming to me like that, demanding he show you his job. This is a downer for me. Next time don't put yourself out there like you're all that!" the Usher said abruptly.

Steve had a recent encounter with a man out in Maryland that used work with at the White House. "Hey Steve, where have you been? I haven't seen you in a long time" said the White House colleague. "You know I retired back in 2002. It's now 2016 so I've been retired for the last 14 years," said Steve. "I've been spending a lot of time with my family," he said. "Man you should be glad you're not working down here now, everything has changed," said the colleague. "You remember all the chandeliers and windows that you used to keep so clean? Well, no one is doing them now; they only call in contractors. When one chandelier gets dirty a contractor comes in and cleans it. And the window washer that they have only washes the windows on the inside because he is afraid and doesn't know how to get on the outside!" All in a breath he exclaimed.

(Courtesy of White House Photographers)   (Courtesy of Stewart C. Stevens Sr.)

ALL-AROUND GOOD GUY

Stewart Calvin was an "All-Around" good natured person. He liked pitching horse-shoes, playing checkers, bowling (as we know from the "Happy Hookers" White House Bowling team), and gardening.

It's recalled, before the White House experience that daddy took us three older children to the Commerce Departments Aquarium many years ago. "At the age of seven or eight years old, the first three would frequent the National Aboretum off of New York Avenue, Washington, DC". Mom was expecting and we all would go bowling with daddy.

When Stewart Calvin first started at the White House, he was driving his Brown and White Station Wagon Sudan. This was the family car for Marie and all 5 of the children. Initially, Stewart Calvin didn't work as many hours and later in life he picked up more hours. However, such was not the case during this time in his life. He was younger and a little more carefree. "Stewart Calvin would drive for hours with his family taking them 8 -12 hours to Atlanta, Georgia to see his brother and to Charlotte, North Carolina to see Marie's family. These were such memorable times!" "Marie was delighted to take these road trips and see her family in North Carolina too!" she recalls.

(Courtesy of Lynetta Stevens)

A few years after "STEVE' had embarked on a White House Career, as the hours picked up and he was sure of it, he purchased a black Cadillac. The more time went by and he could afford it he purchased another one. He finally started purchasing the Cadillac brand. He had a few black Cadillacs, and finally purchased a green Cadillac Eldorado. He kept his automobiles spotless, shiny and always waxed. The car, the rims and all. Even the interior was clean and spotless. Steve wanted to ensure it was something he was proud to drive around and show. This is especially true since he had an assigned parking space behind the White House. He was delighted when his co-workers wanted to inspect his ride and say, "Hey man; that sure is a nice ride you got there!! What year is your Caddy?! Stewart was a Cadillac man! I used to joke with him sometime and call him "Show Boat".

(Courtesy of Lynetta Stevens)

*Prior to owning a Cadillac, "**STEVE**" drove his 80s styled designer van with tinted windows, 8-track tape player that he consistently played country music; switching back to soul and R&B. In particular his favorite was Charlie Pride. He kept his van spotless and with good music!. The van was very unique especially so due to the black tire rim with a custom designed and painted Pink Rose that read, "**MARIE**" mounted to the back. Such was the style back then. He stored the custom designed tire cover in* *his garage for many years....it was a keepsake reminder of his MARIE especially after her loss.*

(Courtesy of Lynetta Stevens)

(Courtesy of Great-Granddaughter of Stewart C. Stevens Sr.)

(Courtesy of Lynetta Stevens)

Stewart, never expected anyone to give him anything, he put his time in and worked hard!!! Yet if he gave; he only expected others to treat him the same. Reciprocation is fair. Birds and fish both reciprocate! Fish swim in an aquarium and entertain and birds are beautiful, just feed them and they continue to return, sing, talk (if they are parrots). Nature has its own way of giving back. Which brings me to his love of birds and fish. Stewart was a nature-loving man!

The love of the birds and the daily bird watching and feedings was what he liked to do. Stewart was a nature person and sitting from his deck to enjoy the tranquility while admiring his yard was very rewarding. Taking trips to the store to purchase bird seeds to attract Red Cardinals and Blue Jays was the weekly highlights. On rare occasions, he would notice Wood peckers and Hummingbirds!

Stewart liked the sport of fishing and anything that revolved around fish, was an infatuation. He enjoyed the sport of fishing. Even if he didn't catch anything; (of course it was better if he did) which was a delight. He enjoyed going out on a boat; he often talked of getting a boat as a younger man. The hobby of maintaining and caring for a school of fish, and upkeep of his beautiful Aquarium made Stewart happy. The way he had the aquarium all decorated was quite elaborate and it was a great conversation piece!

(Courtesy of Stewart C Stevens Sr.)

As personally recalled, as a younger woman and while dating, a young man had the opportunity to meet Stewart. The guy admired the fish aquarium and how beautifully decorated it was. He went on to ask Stewart, what kind of fish they were. Stewart replied, they're Piranhas man". The young guy said, "They're so large Mr. Stevens, what exactly do you feed them?" He replied, "Oh, anything we don't like". It was amazing how fast he left, we never saw that guy again". "This event was hilarious! This is a fond memory for me."

Outside of family life, these were his pass-times.

(Courtesy of Lynetta Stevens)

Stewart was still fishing up into his later life. Stewart Calvin and his son fished often in younger years.

After the pandemic and upon losing his firstborn son-- Stewart took to a long-time and close neighbor as a brother. They developed a great friendship; they both liked fishing!

Stewart Calvin's love for dogs goes way back. When Stewart was younger father, he had a set of pet Pekingese dogs, as recalled. Stewart Calvin mated them and we had a whole family of little Pekingese pups. Penny was red and pretty, snappy and mean. But she was adored! Stewart would walk her and the pups on most brisk fall days, with his brown felt Tam pulled to the side of his head. He often wore the Tam as a younger man, smoking his cigar or pipe, they all took a stroll. Marie would ask, "Where you going Calvin?" I'm going out with" Penny and the pups". It's evident they were sold eventually, they left one by one. He was developing an entrepreneur spirit of dog breeding. Stewart liked a little Collie dog, Princess and a few other pets. She came after he had started working for the White House. Stewart wanted a dog for companionship in his later years, but unfortunately he was never able to get one. Stewart often talked about the Presidential pet dogs.

Stewart liked one of the family pet dogs and often frequented the family pets..

(Courtesy of Lynetta Stevens)

(Courtesy of Stewart C. Stevens Sr.)

This is what one of his White House colleagues said of Stewart, and I quote

"Stewart was a good friend and wonderful human-being. We share many wonderful times and he was a man of wisdom. Not only was he good at his profession, he was a skilled fisherman. Stewart worked for himself, not against himself. He kept those chandeliers, windows and other glassware around the White House spotless."

(Courtesy of Jose' Brown)

THE JOURNEY: A WORK IN PROGRESS

The historical Journey towards publicity started as (Daughter and Author) with permission of Stewart to publish his life story. As he verbally expressed the story of his life, she simultaneously wrote of it.

"It is revered as a magnificent life story and a great idea for which I have great passion". This was especially so since initially Stewart was hired to take on washing 147 windows; until he volunteered to clean and polisher one Chandelier. From that day on this became his specialty, "The Chandeliers".

(Courtesy of Lynetta Stevens)

In the early spring of 2016, the book, "The White House Chandeliers, My Experience While Working for Seven U.S. Presidents" was published and circulated throughout, bookstores, online, Meet and Greet Book Events (at churches), museums, local and well known book stores and community events. One community book event, my two sisters attended.

Initially, contact was made to the Washington Post. The Post was eager to learn of the White House Chandelier Polisher (During an earlier time in history, The Chandeliers were lowered from the vaults onto the floors for 4-5 staffers to clean and polish the gigantic chandeliers) of the U.S. White House.

Later in the year October 6, 2016 to be exact the article "A Sparkling Career" was published in the Washington Post as written by a Washington Post reporter. Following this, CSPAN Book TV staff contacted Stewart and spoke with him regarding a book interview. On December 17th -18th, 2016, CSpan arrived at the home of Stewart C. Stevens, Sr. and staffers filmed the interview of Mr. Stevens! He was really excited and optimistic that his story was getting exposure. Stewart called to notify his family and friends. to let everyone know. This later led to multiple interviews including an in- person sit down interview in February 2017 for Black History month, Fox5. Technically, the interview appeared about 6 months later due to scheduling.

A phone call came in again in February 2017, requesting that Stewart would interview with him on a local TV station (PG's CTV) in Maryland during Black History month. Stewart was becoming more and more optimistic and he enjoyed telling his story. He enjoyed being filmed and televised. Then of course months later, The Smithsonian Folklore Museum, The Smithsonian African-American Museum. When Stewart received a call from (NBC4), he was all in!! Stewart even had an advertisement at the Eastern Market Metro Station, Washington, DC

(Courtesy of Lynetta Stevens)

Book events consisted of TC Wlliams High School, Virginia, Smithsonian African-American Institute, SE Washington, DC, Reginald F. Lewis, Museum, Baltimore, Benjamin Banneker Museum, MD and various other places within the community. The Cheverly Community in Prince Georges County, MD while involved in interviews, we were simultaneously doing book orders!

As recalled, in early 2018 Stewart had a short admittance at George Washington Hospital. Oh "Wow he exclaimed, that's one of the best hospitals! That's where President Reagan went during his attempted assassination!" It was recalled how Stewart was telling all the doctors and nurses how he cleaned The Chandeliers, of the White House for 34 years, and beginning with President Nixon. He was ecstatic and they were surprised. "Oh yeah man", I did it all and all the windows too!"

Sometime later in 2018 after Stewart had recuperated and a few other YouTube videos were produced for a video interview of Stewart. People had started calling Stewart, "THE CHANDELIER MAN"

(Courtesy of Lynetta Stevens)

During all Stewart's TV and You Tube appearance, he never failed mentioning his beloved wife, Marie. He always spoke of her with terms of endearment for her. Missing her and talking of her was a given.

(Courtesy of Lynetta Stevens)

In July 2019, The Play, The White House Chandeliers was produced by none other than Stewart and Lynetta. A few staffers of the White House Historical Association came to support the play as books were being sold with Stewart Calvin Stevens' Sr. original signature. It was the first of what we thought would be many, but such was not the case.

We were going strong and then the pandemic of 2020 hit which shut things down for furtherance of either another play or book signing event-- no longer able to get out for more exposure. The 2020 pandemic forever changed life. Also due to the pandemic, Stewart lost a few close and immediate family members. His first son and his first great-grandson. This was such a blow.

Unfortunately, grief set in and he lost his vigor...things were not the same. However, once the White House Quarterly publication, "Furnishing the White House: The Decorative Arts Collection was published and an article of Stewart appeared, he was trying to bounce back and pick up to where they had left off pre-pandemic. The White House Historical Association did a voice over recording of him. He was really excited and it was all exciting!

(Courtesy of Lynetta Stevens)

(Courtesy of Lynetta Stevens)

At his book signing – smiling and happy

FORWORD ON THE U.S. PRESIDENTS

Here you are Stewart C. Stevens, with your White House staff group photo, (in the middle); one can spot you from a distance (Center), because you are Unique. You are the only one I noticed with a Bow-Tie on in your White House family photo. Uniquely Yours,

ALTHOUGH I WORKED FOR seven United States Presidents, each one of them entirely different, yet similar as well in some ways. I had a lot of respect for each and every one of them. The collection of gifts from each over the years is voluminous in size, consisting of huge collections of photos, portraits, souvenirs, wood products from White House original wood, an ink pen signed by Nancy Reagan, Presidential vases and other artifacts and exhibits of interest. Every one of the Presidents gave me portraits for each year they were in Office during my tenure.

The White House Residential Staff 1988

(Courtesy of Stewart C. Stevens Sr.)

While working for each President, I felt as if we were all one family for the eight hours or so of my shift. Typically, whatever affected the President or the first family or whatever he was dealing with during his time in office affected the entire staff. Be it a time of war, special or sentimental moments such as the passing of a loved one, or any other crisis affecting them personally, or any adverse crises affecting the country, it also affected the White House staff.

(Courtesy of Stewart C. Stevens Sr.)

One other thing that affected the White House staff was the end of the term of a President. Once a Presidential term ends for one of the Presidents, you feel such remorse and sadness. For four or eight years or whatever the case may be, as a White House employee you developed a close bond to the President and the First Family. Especially when assisting with packing, you felt a sadness because if the President was departing, you felt as if you were losing a family member. Behind the wrought iron security gates is your eight-hours or at times 16-hours or more family. It's your world and you are representing it. It is your mission to impress the outside world and tourists coming to visit. As a White House worker you feel such pride because your home is on display.

It has to be pretty and must show polished furniture, waxed and glossy flooring, cleaned and polished chandeliers and definitely no cobwebs – you take such pride in it. It goes beyond your paycheck and is more as if it were your own home and your work being on display, so you go beyond your call of duty.

In the White House world, everyone plays a part, as in an orchestra and everyone playing his own instrument. Everyone is responsible for the part that they play in their performance of doing his or her job. You feel that you all are brothers and sisters working within a family. It's a family type of environment.

(Courtesy of White House Photographer, 1988)

For example, there was one guy named Dale that worked there for 40 years, and he took care of everyone that came in with pets; grooming them and feeding them. And so it is for every other profession within the White House.

On holidays in particular, it was down-time because the Presidents were on personal travel. We still did our jobs but we were not under the microscope or on our guards as much as when the First Family was away.

Whenever they had a State Dinner I often assisted with Operations. An incident happened one night when we had to take a special box into the State Dining Room for the news anchorman to take pictures of the President giving a speech. The news people had to wait half an hour. Two of us while dressed in tuxedos had to stand in the Red Room by the two doors leading into the State Dining Room. We would keep the doors closed until the dinner was over and then we would open the doors so the news people could get up on the box while the President was giving the speech. We would have to slip in real fast to get this box in for the news anchorman to get in and take pictures.

PRESIDENT RICHARD M. NIXON

Administration: 1969-1974

PRESIDENT RICHARD M. NIXON was elected as President of the United States in 1968. In the year 1969, President Richard M. Nixon was sworn in as the 37th President of the United States of America. The First Lady was Patricia Nixon who was a soft and elegant First Lady. This was the first President for whom I worked. Not starting employment at the beginning of the Nixon Presidency, but rather hired in the middle of his term in 1970, left me at a disadvantage of not forming as close of a relationship as I did with some of the other Presidents. Although I did not have much familiarity with him, and did not see him as much, he was a very nice President. I recall that every Christmas, President Richard Nixon would give all of the employees a gift for each of their children. I certainly remember bringing a toy for each of my four children at that time.

President Richard M. Nixon, as I remember, had two daughters of whom he was very proud. The oldest was Julie and her younger sister was Patricia, referred to as "Tricia." Tricia was the first young lady to be married in the Rose Garden, and what a wedding it was! President Nixon's daughter Julie served as her sister's Maid of Honor. It was a rainy day, but a beautiful wedding! I can recall President Nixon riding in the limousine with Tricia.

(Courtesy of Stewart C. Stevens Sr.& White House Photographers)

On December 21, 1970, Elvis Presley visited President Richard M. Nixon at the White House. President Nixon made Elvis a "Federal Agent-at-Large" in the Bureau of Narcotics and Dangerous Drugs. Elvis gave President Nixon gifts, including a Colt 45 pistol and family photos that Presley brought with him to the Oval Office. I was not working here at this time, but it was often talked about by many staff members.

Under the Nixon Administration, there was an event on the National Mall in May 1974 called *Human Kindness Day*. There were problems from the start. Organizers had trouble getting the sound system to work because spectators were sitting on the equipment. There was a lot of rioting during the *Human Kindness Day* event in 1974. However, I was working on the inside of the White House on that day. But I recall that this was going on during this time, and I thought it may be something significant as a part of history.

President Nixon gave me one Rembrandt portrait of President Thomas Jefferson. He gave me two other portraits that were not Rembrandt, however beautiful, of President Abraham Lincoln and James Monroe.

It was during the Nixon Administration, in 1974, when I found some confidential documents and a check for $14.5 million in the

Treasury corridor while walking over to the Treasury Department on my lunch break and was rewarded $50. Once taxes were deducted, I received $40.

President Nixon was impeached, although he resigned before it actually happened, in 1974 and this I do recall. There was a certain chill within the walls of the White House around the time of the impeachment proceedings. "President Nixon will be leaving the Presidency," someone had announced to the staff. On the day that President Nixon was leaving, the weather was fair and quite sunny; it was a sad day in the history of the United States of America. Everyone was standing on the Truman Balcony when the President made the victory sign, threw up both hands and boarded Air Force One. We all waived at him. There were staff members that actually stood there and cried as Air Force One took off into thin air. The President that we once knew will be remembered for generations to come.

"Hello, Stevens," said Mrs. Bender, the housekeeper. "Good morning Mrs. Bender," he said. "How's your new job coming along?" "Everything is good Mrs. Bender," said Stevens. "I'm trying to keep on top of my many assignments and cleaning all the chandeliers. You are a very nice housekeeper, Mrs. Bender, and I really enjoy you taking me under your wing," said Steve.

It was a drizzling day with light showers as Patricia Nixon was getting ready for her wedding. "Hi Riley, what did you need my help with?" "Well, Stevens, if you can grab a few chairs for me, we are getting ready for Tricia's wedding," said Riley. "Sure Riley, I got all my work done with the chandeliers so I'm glad to help, and I've also worked to complete the stage while working with Operations. You know me, I am very versatile in helping with many things," said Stewart. "Is this the first time that any of the daughters had been married in the Rose Garden?" He asked. "Yeah, I think so," Riley said. "The President seems very excited about his daughter getting married in the Rose Garden."

"Hello everyone, the President will be leaving. Have you all heard?" "Yeah, we heard and it's really sad to see him have to go."

"Hi Stevens, are you going out to waive good-bye to the President?" "Yes I will be right out there. Where's the rest of the staff?" Said, Steve. "I'm sorry I wasn't able to know him better."

PRESIDENT GERALD R. FORD

Administration: 1974-1977

PRESIDENT GERALD R. FORD was elected in 1973 and sworn into the White House as the 38th President of the United States of America in 1974. He was the second President for whom I worked. The First Lady was Betty Ford. President Ford was a pleasant and easy going President and the First Lady was quiet and rather shy.

In May1975 during his Administration, *Human Kindness Day* was held in Washington DC on the National Mall. The Washington Post reported that about 55,000 people attended *Human Kindness Day III* and that 24 people were arrested on assault and robbery charges.

President Ford really liked to play golf. Unfortunately, he would always hit someone with the ball. He had a wonderful family. His wife was Betty Ford and they had four wonderful children.

In 1974, New York City avoided bankruptcy when President Gerald R. Ford signed a $2.3 billion loan, and the unemployment rate in US reached 9.2%, and a recession was recognized by the President. The United States pulled out of Cambodia. I did not have much interaction with President Gerald Ford, but I do remember that he was a peacemaker and he had a wonderful family. He gave me several watercolor paintings signed by him.

"Good morning, Mr. President." "Good morning, Mr. Stevens. The Chandeliers are looking good. I'll see that the Chief Usher and Chief of Housekeeping are notified of how pleased I am with the work you are doing," said President Ford. "Thank you Mr. President," Stewart said.

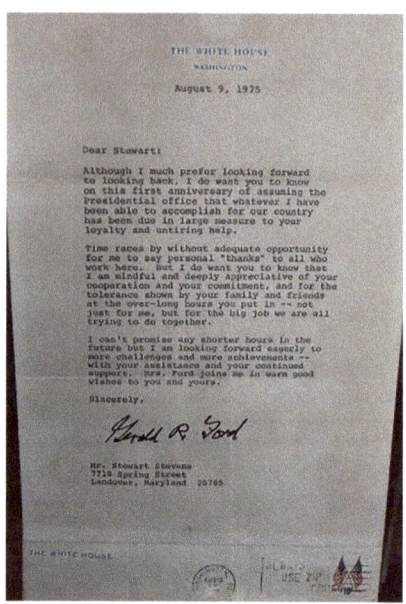

(Courtesy of Stewart C. Stevens Sr.)

After leaving work one evening, he came through the door and was aggravated more than normal. "Hi honey, how was your day?" "It was wonderful until I tried to make my way home. The commute was terrible due to an event down on the Washington Mall." As everyone was anxiously awaiting their father's return home to give a report on how many chandeliers and light globes he had cleaned and polished for the day, they were baffled at how drained he seemed. They noticed there was a difference in him compared to most other days. "Children go get your homework done or complete your chores, your father needs time to wind down," Marie said. "Sure Mama," the children replied. Marie was very intuitive of her husband's changing mood, knowing he is typically upbeat and happy.

Later, "Hi Daddy, did you hear about the event called Human Kindness Day where groups of singers came and the people started fighting and rioting?" "No, I have not heard of the day's events because I've been busy attending to my job within the White House and not really in tune to other things going on outside on the Washington Mall, but I know something was going on in downtown Washington DC due to the traffic congestion, bottles, trash and paper scattered all over the place. I believe there was some rioting going on and it really surprised me," he said. "It took my mind back to the day Dr. King was assassinated." "Daddy, Mama and I have been watching the news and all and it's terrible," his daughter said. Marie, chimed in, "Yes Baby, what happened at the event was so disgraceful that I've decided to address my thoughts about it by writing an article to the Washington Post. I feel so lucky to be protected in the comfort of our home and caring for the family during the day, which allows me time to keep up with world events. And I am definitely on the up and up of what's going on around me," Marie said. "Writing an article to address these concerns for more unity and acceptance of others seems like a great idea to me." "It sounds like a good idea to me too, Mama!" their daughter said. "My girls!" he exclaimed.

(Courtesy of Stewart C. Stevens, Sr.)

PRESIDENT JAMES E. CARTER, JR

Administration: 1977-1980

PRESIDENT JAMES E. CARTER was elected in 1976. In 1977, he was sworn in as the 39th President of the United States of America. The First Lady was Rosalyn Carter. First Lady Rosalyn Carter was very dedicated in her ministry and was supportive to her husband as his calling was to God and the people. President Carter was referred to as "Jimmy" and was the third President for whom I worked.

Each morning at 6:00 am promptly, President Carter would go to the Oval Office carrying his Bible with him. I would be there to open the door for him. He would always say "Good morning Steve." It made me feel very good to have the President of the United States address me by my name. It was exemplary of any President to put a name to a face and treat an employee with respect for his person and not only the job that he was hired to do. Although all the Presidents and the First Ladies knew what an excellent job I did when they saw the Chandeliers sparkling and the windows cleaned, they were rather amazed too.

I can recall the Camp David Accords, signed by President Jimmy Carter, Egyptian President Al Sadat, and Israeli Prime Minister Menachem Begin in September 1978. A framework was established for a historic peace treaty concluded between Israel and Egypt in March 1979. President Carter and the US Government played leading roles in creating the opportunity for this agreement to occur. From the start of his Administration, Carter and his Secretary of State, Cyrus Vance, pursued intensive negotiations with Arab and Israeli leaders, hoping to reconvene the Geneva Conference, which had been established in December 1973 to seek an end to the Arab- Israeli dispute. I remember when President Carter warned Americans to make profound changes in their oil consumption. Due to the gas shortage, there were gas lines and people were fighting over gas. During the Carter Administration, I remember that in 1978 Cardinal Karol Wojtyla became Pope John Paul II. I recall the visit of Pope John Paul II when he visited the White House and met with President Jimmy Carter and the First Lady Rosalyn Carter in the Yellow Oval Room.

(Courtesy of Stewart C. Stevens Sr.)

(Courtesy of Stewart C. Stevens Sr.)

In 1979, the Iranian oil prices increased around the world and the public begin to panic. When they panicked and started buying more oil and gas, things got worse.

During the Carter Administration there was a tense and anxious feeling in the air when the United States troops were taken hostage in Iran and President Carter had to try to figure out how to get the troops back. President Carter tried to free the US hostages in Iran, but it was a failed attempt because the helicopters were not equipped to deal with the sand. The sand came into the engines of the helicopters and caused them to crash. Towards the end of the Carter Administration, the Iranians wanted to release the hostages but they delayed it until the new President came. The new President was Ronald Reagan. Ronald Reagan was in office for a brief time and then they released the hostages. This, of course, became a victory for Reagan. The victory would have eventually come to the United States under the Carter Administration had there been more time during the Carter Presidency.

What I admired about President Carter was how, after his Presidency, he came back to the Washington DC area in the Southeast neighborhood not far from where I grew up to design and build affordable homes for lower income families in order that they take advantage of having home ownership. He gave back to the American people. President Jimmy Carter later turned to diplomacy and advocacy, for which he was awarded the Nobel Prize for Peace in 2002. One of my favorite books by President Jimmy Carter is the *Virtues of Aging*. One historical fact pertaining to President Carter is that he was the first United States President to be born in a hospital.

Under the Carter Administration, I was given a picture of his mother, Lillian Carter, his only daughter, Amy Carter, and a family photo of his entire family.

"Good morning, Steve," said the President. "Good morning Mr. President!" "How are you today?" "I'm great. I've got that door for you, President Carter." "Thank you so much, Steve! I'm on my way to the Oval Office and I've got the Good Book in my hand for today's assignments. I want to follow His agenda not my own agenda. I know He will hold me responsible and accountable for this high calling as the President of the United States of America and I promised Him that I would do my best!" "That makes two of us Mr. President! I'm aiming to do my best with what He gave me to do because I know that He placed me here at the White House," said Steve. "You always address me so nicely Sir and I appreciate that," said Steve. "That is because your face is so pleasant and I notice you doing such a wonderful job. I feel we have a connection other than the work that we are called to do here at the White House, so I place a name with your face." "Thank you, Mr. President. We are basically working for the same Boss," said Steve. I truly appreciate that you respect people for who they are, Mr. President." "Why thank you, Mr. Steve!" said President, Carter.

On a cold wintry day in December, the staff was very excited to be going on a surprise trip. "Good morning all," said Mrs. Crans-Limerick. "The President wants to take you all on a surprise trip to Camp David. "Camp David!" said, Steve. "That is wonderful." "Well, Steve, would you like to go with the group to Camp David?" asked Mrs. Crans-Limerick. "Yes! I sure would like to go." "Well you all can get changed into your clothes and get ready to board the bus," she said. "Hey man this is awesome; I can't wait to go see where the Presidents hold their meetings," said Steve.

We got there approximately three to four hours later and everyone was getting off the bus. "This is really a kind and thoughtful gesture by President Carter," Steve said, and all the staff chimed in, "Yeah it sure is nice of him. He's such a sensitively-kind President, we never would have had the chance to go to Camp David!" "Well, alright so this is where all the Presidents go to retreat. It's really a welcoming retreat, beautiful scenery and all."

"Ok, folks, enjoy!" shouted the bus driver to the group. All of the staff went over to the Dining Hall where they were set up to serve dinner. "Hello everyone," said the one of the officers of the Navy staff. "We are here to serve you. You all serve every day and now we want to serve you, and by the way the White House Butlers are not doing the serving – we are. So take a seat, make yourselves at home, and leave the rest to us," said one of the gentlemen from the Navy staff. The round tables were set for six to a table and the tablecloths and china were so fancy, as if fit for a King. President Carter sat at the table that was closest to Steve. "Well hello everyone. I am so elated to have you here and glad that you all were able to make it!" said the President. "They've prepared a nice meal and the food is delicious, but I really don't drink wine," he said. "Would you like have my wine Steve?" "Yes Sir! Mr. President, he said. I'll take your wine; I cannot ever say no to the President!" And everyone laughed. They talked about it the next day and it became the conversation piece of that day. "Hey Steve, you drank the President's wine! Said one of the housekeeping staff. "Well, I look at it this way: You never say no to the President!" said Steve, and they all laughed again.

One day as Pope John Paul II came and left, I was thinking about him and the photographer approached me and we started up a conversation.

"Steve, you talk so much about the Pope as if you have an interest in him." "I do have an interest. I like the Pope and I am really intrigued by him. He's interested in reaching out to the people and being a servant, much like our very own President Carter who reaches out to the American people and surrounding communities," said Steve. "Well Stevens, I am intrigued by you and how you sparked such an interest. You're a good guy, and as the photographer I want you to take a short trip to my area with me; I have some pictures of the Pope, and I'll see that you get a few." "Well, thank you Bill. I will keep these for years to come!" "Did you give pictures to anyone of the others, Bill?" "No, this is a special for you. We've been working together for such a long time and I like you." "Thank you, Bill, for capturing some nice moments of me in photos. I know my family will treasure these photos in years to come. You are really talented and I appreciate it," said Steve. "You're welcome. You're very welcome," he said.

(Courtesy of Stewart C. Stevens, Sr.)

PRESIDENT RONALD W. REGAN

Administration: 1980-1989

IN 1979, PRESIDENT RONALD W. Regan was elected. In 1980, he was sworn in as the 40th President of the United States of America. As a two-Term President, he was the fourth President for whom I worked. President Regan was referred to as "The Gipper." He was a movie star before he became President and the Governor of California. The First Lady was Nancy Reagan, who was also a movie star years ago, and they even made pictures together. First Lady, Nancy Reagan, was a very graceful and wise lady from what I can remember. She helped her husband make sound decisions as the President. She was especially supportive to her husband in times of crisis and she gave him words of wisdom before he made any major decisions. I recall an incident that occurred in the country. Someone asked him, "Mr. President do you think they are honest?" He replied, "Trust them but cut the cards."

(Courtesy of Stewart C. Stevens Sr.)

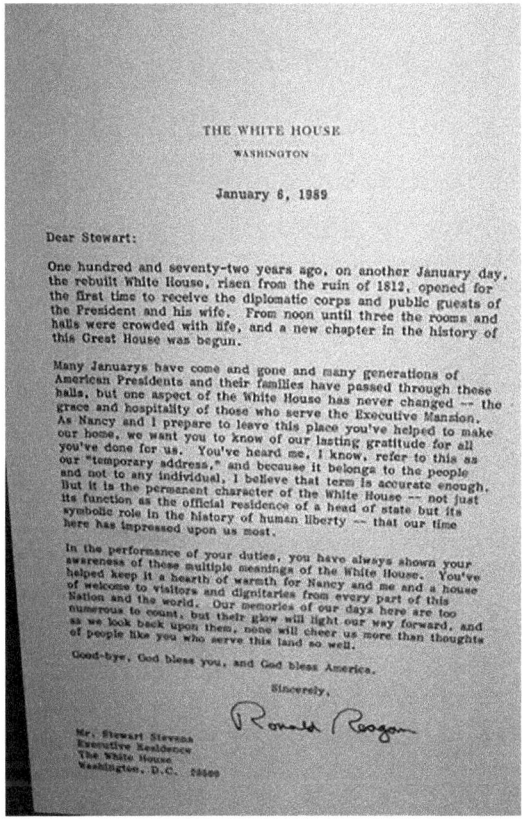

THE WHITE HOUSE
WASHINGTON

January 6, 1989

Dear Stewart:

One hundred and seventy-two years ago, on another January day, the rebuilt White House, risen from the ruin of 1812, opened for the first time to receive the diplomatic corps and public guests of the President and his wife. From noon until three the rooms and halls were crowded with life, and a new chapter in the history of this Great House was begun.

Many Januarys have come and gone and many generations of American Presidents and their families have passed through these halls, but one aspect of the White House has never changed -- the grace and hospitality of those who serve the Executive Mansion. As Nancy and I prepare to leave this place you've helped to make our home, we want you to know of our lasting gratitude for all you've done for us. You've heard me, I know, refer to this as our "temporary address," and because it belongs to the people and not to any individual, I believe that term is accurate enough. But it is the permanent character of the White House -- not just its function as the official residence of a head of state but its symbolic role in the history of human liberty -- that our time here has impressed upon us most.

In the performance of your duties, you have always shown your awareness of these multiple meanings of the White House. You've helped keep it a hearth of warmth for Nancy and me and a house of welcome to visitors and dignitaries from every part of this Nation and the world. Our memories of our days here are too numerous to count, but their glow will light our way forward, and as we look back upon them, none will cheer us more than thoughts of people like you who serve this land so well.

Good-bye, God bless you, and God bless America.

Sincerely,

Ronald Reagan

Mr. Stewart Stevens
Executive Residence
The White House
Washington, D.C. 20500

(Courtesy of Ronald Regan Presidential Library)

In 1981 as I recall, the Air Traffic Controllers had a strike that caused chaos, and President Reagan fired them. Yes, I do remember the strikes of Air Traffic Controllers. I also remember President Reagan's speech at the Berlin Wall where he said, as if he was giving an order, "Mr. Mikhail Gorbachev, *tear down this wall.*"

One year, President Reagan invited Michael Jackson down to the White House for lunch. He and the First Lady, Nancy Reagan, were very hospitable towards Michael Jackson, and she really enjoyed his style and music. The press was all around and Michael Jackson came out and grabbed himself as he usually does, waved his hands with his famous white glove, and the crowd just went wild hollering and screaming.

I recall hearing all around the White House and on the news that during the assassination attempt on President Reagan he wanted to go back to the White House but the Secret Service rushed him to George Washington University Hospital since they did not know if he had been shot or not. When they arrived at George Washington University Hospital, they rushed him to the Emergency Room and immediately they started examining him.

They found a little bit of blood coming from his mouth. They had to x-ray him to determine whether he had been shot or not. As it turned out he had actually been shot. He did not realize how close to death he was. When they discovered that he had been shot they prepped him so they could perform emergency surgery. But, before they actually started operating he raised his head and asked the doctors, "Are you Republicans or Democrats?" A few minutes later the First Lady Nancy Reagan arrived to the hospital and she hurried right in. They were so much in love and Mrs. Reagan worried that she would lose him.

A few days later, President Reagan was up and waving out the hospital window. As a result, when George Washington Hospital decided to expand and build a new wing, they named it in honor of President Ronald Reagan. When President Reagan was shot, it affected the entire staff. There was a sadness and anxiety in the atmosphere. Everybody was worried because they thought a lot of President Reagan. They did not know whether he was going to live or die.

Meanwhile, Press Secretary Brady was shot twice in the head and it paralyzed him for life. As a result the "Brady" bill was passed to take the handguns off the street, but it never happened. Mr. Hinckley was the assassin that attempted to take President Reagan's life. The removal of handguns was not successful. They are still trying to get the handguns off the street.

When President Reagan returned back to White House he was also waving out of his bedroom window to the large crowd of people cheering for him, letting them know that he was doing fine. Although he was the President, he still had a movie star personality!

Under Reagan's administration there was a cork floor in the Oval Office that had served six Presidents. The cork was starting to crack. President Reagan decided that he wanted to put a new floor in the Oval Office. I helped the carpenters bust up the old cork floor and we replaced it with hardwood flooring. President Reagan liked the floor so much that he sent each one of us a piece of the cork floor in a hard plastic container, thanking us for a job well done.

It is also noted that during the Reagan Administration the outside windows of the Oval Office had so many coats of paint that the painters had to use a torch to burn the paint off the window frames before repainting. As a result of the torch being too hot, the windows caught on fire. Afterwards the fire department was called in to put the fire out. As the firefighters came in to put the fire out, they had to drag their hose across the Oval Office floor. The Chief Ushers did not approve of the firefighters dragging the hose into the Oval Office. They had to put down drop cloth to prevent the fireman from destroying the Presidential Oval Rug on the floor. The staff of the West Wing had to come in and clean up the mess.

"Hello, Mr. President. I've watched you in many movies and one in particular with Nancy Reagan many years ago," said Stewart. "I hear the Air Traffic controllers are going on strike," he said. "Good morning Steve," said Mrs. Crans-Limerick. "Hello, Mrs. Crans- Limerick." "Steve, we will have a project for you to assist the carpenter staff with. The President is requesting that cork floor in the Oval Office be replaced with wood floors. The cork floor has served six administrations and it's time that it is removed due to the cork cracking and all. It doesn't serve the White House very well and it's not appealing to President anymore. You know the tourists come through from time to time and new wood would do the White House justice." said Mrs. Crans-Limerick. "Hey there Mrs. Crans-Limerick," called out one of the carpenter's supervisors, "Is that Steve?" "It sure is," she said. "When are we going to have the meeting to discuss the new project of replacing the floors in the Oval Office" asked the supervisor. "I'm speaking with him about that now, so your timing is perfect." She said. "Great, we'll need some extra help on this project." As they spoke, Steve agreed, "Sure I am available to work with your carpenters and appreciate the opportunity," he called out.

In the coming weeks, the new wood was installed. "Hello, everyone!" President Reagan said in a gleeful and cheery voice. "I really like that wood flooring you all installed. It looks fantastic. I have a piece of the original cork that was removed and would like to give you all a piece as a souvenir. The cork has served through six US Presidents and as a part of history, I think you would like to keep it since it is historical." President Reagan handed every one that worked on the project a piece of cork in a plastic container. "You all did such a wonderful job, and Nancy is very pleased!" The President said. They all thanked him and returned to the next project.

"Everyone please come to the conference room," the housekeeper said. "The President has been shot! There is a televised viewing in the conference room of what just happened," she said. All eyes welled up with sullen faces, confused and dazed faces, disappointed and shocked faces staring around the room. "Oh, my Lord," Someone called out, "What's going to happen to our President?" They listened awhile with an eager ear as the anchorman announced on CSPAN news that President Ronald Reagan had been immediately rushed to the George Washington University Hospital Emergency Room, which was the closest hospital located on Pennsylvania Avenue, NW. There was a sudden anxiety and chilling effect within the White House. "Please help him; we cannot bear to lose our President," they mumbled in disbelief. The chaplain was offering support for anyone that wanted to visit the chapel to have a few words of prayer for the fallen President. The President was in critical condition, meanwhile, the news reporting stated, "The President's spokesperson, Mr. Brady, caught a bullet and has had to be rushed to the hospital. A man by the name of Hinckley was arrested for the shooting," said the news reporter. "Oh my, this is such a tragedy!" said the workers. As the day went by, various news stations gave reports on the status of the President and Mr. Brady. "Mr. Brady is in critical condition," said the news reporter. It was later reported that Mr. Brady was paralyzed and would not be able to walk again. "Hey everyone, Brady has been shot and Congress has introduced the Brady bill to remove handguns from off the streets!" "Wow that's interesting. Let's continue and stay tuned to hear the status of our President," they all said. "Mrs. Reagan is all in tears. My heart goes out to her," said Steve.

It was assumed at first that President Reagan had not been shot; however, it was later discovered that the President had been shot. Later a report came across to announce that President Reagan was taken into surgery to try to remove the bullet and there was blood coming from his mouth. The doctors did all that was possible to save his life by preparing him for surgery. "Hi you physicians and surgeons, before you take me under the knife, I have one question I want to ask you," said President Reagan. "What is it Mr. President?" said the attending surgeons. "Are you Republicans or Democrats?" In came the First Lady Nancy Reagan to join beside her husband that she loved for so many years. She rushed right in with the Secret Service. "Please do all that you can to save my husband! God Bless the President and God Bless my husband," she said with a whimper of uncertainty. This was truly a sensitive moment and the surgeons proceeded quickly but cautiously to remove the bullet from President Reagan. Later, after the bullet was removed and the surgery completed, they all just laughed and this became a conversation piece. The staff of George Washing Hospital would jokingly say, "Are you Republican or Democrat?" within the hospital. "Well," said one of the hospital staff, "this has been a bleak moment while serving our President, but we are honored to have been able to treat him here and save his life. He's quite a character and charming person at that, so we took a vote, and whether Democrat or Republican, it didn't make any difference – he is still our American President and the decision was made to name the new wing within the hospital after President Ronald W. Reagan." The GWU staff clapped on that note.

While in his room at the George Washington University Hospital and days after recuperating, President Reagan got out of his hospital bed and went to the windows to wave to the American people. As people gathered around, President Reagan realized how well-loved he was. "Hi, Mr. President! Best wishes and a speedy recovery!" Everyone cried out and waved. He looked out at the crowd as if he was a major star again, starring in a movie!

He did the same thing once he was back at the White House. "Mr. President, Mr. President! Please return to your bed, you must stay on bed rest," cried one of the medical White House Staff." "Oh I'm doing fine, I have such a crowd and audience out here on Pennsylvania Avenue and they love me so! I must get up and wave to the people," said President Reagan, and then later he retired back to his bed.

To Stewart Stevens
With appreciation and best wishes,

(Courtesy of Stewart C. Stevens)

PRESIDENT GEORGE H.W. BUSH

Administration: 1989-1993

IN 1988, PRESIDENT GEORGE Herbert W. Bush was elected. In 1989, he was sworn as the 41st President of the United States of America. He was the fifth President for whom I worked. First Lady Barbara Bush was a woman of strength, and she had plenty of pride as the Matron of her family. She was a supportive wife and also a caring mother. Her mothering nature carried over to the White House staff.

Under the George H.W. Bush Administration, Operation Desert Storm took place in Iraq and Kuwait. The Iraqi President, Saddam Hussein, invaded Kuwait. Bush was determined to free Kuwait and rallied the United Nations, the United States people and Congress. There was sadness all around when President George H.W. Bush stood in the Oval Office to make the announcement that he would be sending 425,000 American troops over to join with 118,000 troops from allied nations. A 100-hour land battle became known as Desert Storm and it routed Iraq's million man army. The surroundings were very tense as President Bush made this announcement. He did not want to send the men into war but it was something that had to be done. He as the Commander and Chief had to order the troops to be sent as the bill had been passed by Congress to do so.

President Bush was very sociable with the White House staff. He invited all the staff to pick their partners so we could have a horseshoe match. He gave the winners presents like fishing rods and other sports and fishing gear. The catch was that you had to beat him. He was a very honest and decent man, because whether you won or lost he gave out presents.

Boris Yeltsin becomes Russia's first elected President under the George H.W. Bush Administration.

In 1989, President George HW Bush won as the 41st President of the United States of America. In the debates, he hollered out to President Reagan, "Read My Lips: No new taxes," and this became a big slogan during his administration.

As Steve hung around the White House with the safety belt, he noticed President Bush coming in with the Secret Service and he waved. "Hi Steve," said the President as he called out. Later in the day, everyone had a solemn look on their faces. The country was in such a dilemma with the Iraq situation and the decision of whether to involve the United States in the war. It was a tough call, and one only the President could make.

"President Bush will be holding an All Staff meeting within the coming days," said one of the White House staff. Steve came into the main foyer of the North Portico after being on the outside. "Hi, good afternoon," he said. "Why is everyone looking so down?" he thought and started to wonder what was going on. "Man, what is it?" He said. "Last night when I got in it was rather late because I had to work a double. My wife and I looked at the 10:00 news and it doesn't look good between the United States and Iraq," Steve said shaking his head. "Yeah man," said one of his co-workers, "it doesn't look good. They called for an All Staff meeting and the President is going to address next steps for the United States troops." "Oh boy," said Steve, "It is what it is."

Next day, "The President wants to take us to pitch a little horse shoes with him," someone said. "It's been pretty tense around the White House and he needs to unwind, I guess, before making the major announcement concerning Desert Storm."

"Hi everyone, glad you could make it down here in Texas to join me in the game of Horseshoes," said President Bush. "Alright, Mr. Assistant Housekeeper, show me what you got." The horseshoes were pitched. The President pitched and the Assistant Housekeeper pitched. And whatever happened on the golf course stayed on the golf course, and the rest became history.

"Hi, Mrs. Bush," "Hello there, Steve!" she said. "I was glad to hear that you went to my old neighborhood with the Queen of England," Steve noted because it was really something to have the Queen of England visit his community.

(Courtesy of Stewart C. Stevens Sr.)

PRESIDENT WILLIAM J. CLINTON

Administration: 1993-2001

IN 1992, PRESIDENT WILLIAM Jefferson Clinton was elected. In 1993, he was sworn in as the 42nd President of the United States of America. He was the sixth President for whom I worked. President Clinton, referred to as "Bill," was also two-term President. The First Lady, Hillary Rodham Clinton, was a very friendly, professional and a straightforward First Lady. From the very moment President Bill Clinton was sworn into office he had a smooth air about himself as a jazz musician. President Bill Clinton was musically inclined. He made his debut playing the saxophone at his first Inauguration ceremony and pulled the people of the United States of America into his Presidency in a social manner. His favorite saying, when he was elected he told the people, "You got two for the price of one" meaning that he was a lawyer and his wife was a lawyer too.

I remember that in September 1993, Yitzhak Rabin's Israel and Yasser Arafat's PLO signed the peace agreement on the White House lawn. President Bill Clinton did so much to help Black Americans. I remember when Nelson Mandela, the President of South Africa, was invited to the White House in 1994. I saw him as he entered the North Portico to go into meet with President and First Lady Clinton. During the State visit I assisted with the particulars of setting up for his appearance and assisting during the State Dinner. At this time also, the White House had State visits for their Majesties the Emperor and Empress of Japan, and President and Mrs. Yeltsin that I also assisted.

In 1996, Bill Clinton was elected for a second term as the United States President after he defeats Bob Dole. In 1997, Madeleine Albright was appointed as the first female Secretary of State in the United States under the Clinton Administration.

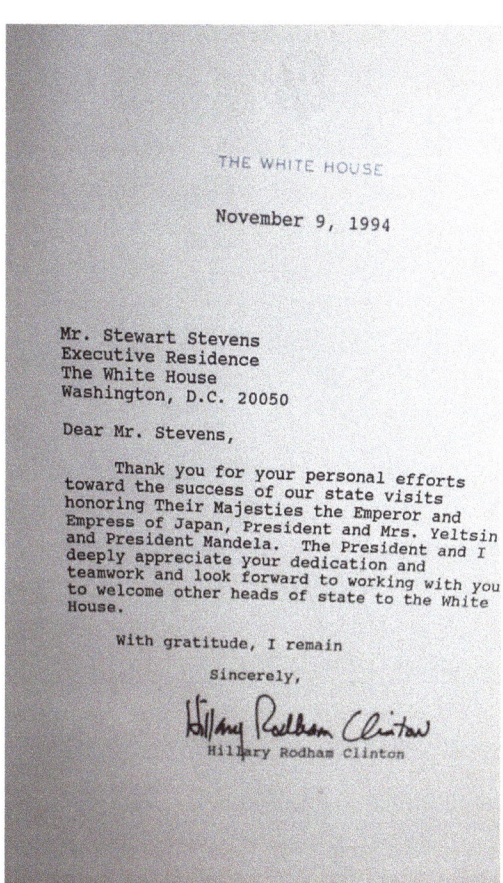

THE WHITE HOUSE

November 9, 1994

Mr. Stewart Stevens
Executive Residence
The White House
Washington, D.C. 20050

Dear Mr. Stevens,

Thank you for your personal efforts toward the success of our state visits honoring Their Majesties the Emperor and Empress of Japan, President and Mrs. Yeltsin and President Mandela. The President and I deeply appreciate your dedication and teamwork and look forward to working with you to welcome other heads of state to the White House.

With gratitude, I remain

Sincerely,

Hillary Rodham Clinton

(Courtesy of Stewart C. Stevens Sr.)

President Clinton was a very friendly and down to earth President. He would ride the elevators with staff and joke around with everybody. The personable relationship between President Clinton and me was truly special. When I lost my mother, President Clinton came down the hall with the Secret Service on the way to the Oval Office and he noticed me there washing windows. President Clinton stopped and came over to me and he said, "Steve, hold your head up because I have been there like you and everything is going to be okay." He and I had a heart-to-heart talk and he explained to me how he was very affected when he lost his mother and how he almost went to pieces because he and his mother were very close as me and my own mother were. We shared a common bond due to our similar and very emotional situations. There was never a President that I worked for that seemed as personable to me during a time of personal crisis and personal loss. Each and every time he passed me, the President stopped to talk. It caused the Secret Service to have to stop each time he stopped to talk. They were probably guessing and wondering why there was such a bond between the two of us. It really made me feel special that he took that time with me. He was much like President Carter in the way he would not pass by me without stopping to speak and address me personally. One of my favorite pictures of President Clinton was the picture that shows him stopping to shake my hand. When I lost my father, President Clinton uplifted me again and spoke some very encouraging words regarding my personal loss.

During the Clinton Administration I lost both my parents; Mrs. Crans-Limerick and Mr. Scouten were very supportive to both me and my family. Mrs. Crans-Limerick came on behalf of the White House to offer condolences and pay her respects during the Memorial ceremonies.

In 1999, President Clinton and the First Lady presented me with a photo plaque addressed to me and my wife on our anniversary celebration.

In the year 2000, President Clinton presented me with a Sterling Silver Millennium Key Chain, which meant a lot to me. While working the residential quarters, there was a special and personal feeling towards President Clinton. It always felt rewarding to have worked under the Clinton Administration, and it was a time of peace without any war.

(Courtesy of Stewart C. Stevens Sr.)

"Hi Mama, how are you and Dad doing? I'm coming up to visit you and Dad; I have a photo of me and the President that I want to give to you." "Well come on up son, we'll be waiting for you." "Alright then Mama, have my cup of tea ready when I get there. It would have been nice if the Queen would have come up to see you few years ago when she came to our neighborhood. You both could have shared a cup of tea." "I would have liked that, Calvin," she said. "There would have been so much publicity!" She said with excitement. "I would have so much to share with my girlfriends too," she laughed.

When Stewart arrived to see his parents, Rachel gladly received him with a big hug and his Dad had a hearty welcome. "Sit on down son, what's been happening?" "Oh, a lot! President Clinton is such a swell guy. He's the President for *all* people, including our people," said Calvin. "What do you mean by that?" asked his Dad. "What I mean is the people in our community, the low to middle class," he said. "He takes a liking to people in our community because he came from humble beginnings and he can relate to everyone. Hey guess what, I got a glimpse of Nelson Mandela, the President from South Africa, when he visited the White House!" "You did? That's really wonderful," Mama said in awe. "My goodness, you actually get the chance to meet some pretty important people." "Yes I do! Pretty exciting," he said. "Here's that picture of me and President Clinton and the First Lady I promised you." "Oh this is something, Stew," she said. "Yes it is," Dad said. "I think, I'll place it right on the wall over there! Hang it up for me honey."

(Courtesy of Stewart C. Stevens Sr.)

"Good afternoon, Steve," said President Clinton. "Hello, Mr. President," said Steve with his head hanging low. "How's everything, Mr. Stevens? Asked the President. "Well, not so good, Mr. President. See, I just lost my mother and it's been very rough on me these past few days. She was a good mother to me and we shared some wonderful times together, so it really hurts me to see my mother go. It's a hurt that I know I will have for some time to come. We lost her days before Thanksgiving and with that coming up, it's just not going to me the same. We are a close-knit family and I'm doing my best to deal with the loss," Steve said. "Mr. President, my brothers and I were the pall bearers at her request. It's tough to have to carry your own mother," he said. "My mother thought a lot of you too," Steve said looking down at his hands as if he was a lost child and didn't know where to go or who to turn to.

"Steve, let me tell you that you are not alone in that personal loss. I cried like a baby when I lost my mother. She and I were very close too. Unfortunately, I can relate to what you are experiencing right now. I nearly went to pieces after losing her. Time will heal it though, but it never goes completely away. Be encouraged and be strong. She would want you to be strong!"

Steve worked hard to get through the personal loss he experienced during the first term of President Clinton's administration. As some time went on it wasn't too long before he had to experience the same loss of his father. "Well, Mr. President, I now have to lay my Dad to rest. We lost him, too, just a few days before Christmas." "Steve, I remember all too well how that felt and I offer many condolences to you and your family. Your Mom and Dad are together now and he's much at rest. You know in your heart that you have been a good son. It's a pleasure knowing you Steve," said the President. "It's a real pleasure knowing you too; you are so much more than a President to me, much much like a friend," Steve said." "Thank you Steve, hang in there and stay strong!"

"Thank you, Mrs. Limerick, for coming to the memorial services. My family appreciates the cards and the flowers," Steve said as Mrs. Crans-Limerick the Housekeeper came to offer her condolences on behalf of the White House.

As time went by, they had a few more short talks together. He treasured these moments and them cherished in his heart.

PRESIDENT GEORGE W. BUSH

Administration: 2001-2009

(Courtesy of Stewart C. Stevens Sr.)

PRESIDENT GEORGE W. BUSH was 43rd President of the United States of America and the seventh Presidential Administration for which I worked. The First Lady, Laura Bush was a reserved and soft-spoken First Lady.

September 11th in 2001 was both historic and catastrophic. This tragic event affected all of the United States of America, but in particular New York City and the Nation's Capital, Washington DC. These two major cities were tremendously affected and families gravely suffered from the tragic loss. There were so many fallen heroes who lost their lives in the line of duty; so many other innocent lives were also claimed during this tragic event. It was during this administration that there was a lot of uncertainty within the walls of the White House. While I was working for George W. Bush's administration I recall the President informing the American people that terrorists had bombed the World Trade Center's Twin Towers in New York City, as well as the Pentagon. The word had got around that a plane was on the way to bomb the White House. Everyone had been ordered to leave the White House except the Secret Service and me. I did not get the word that they were on the way to bomb the White House until the Secret Service told me to run. They told me, "Steve, hurry up and get out of here because they are getting ready to bomb the White House!" That is when I sat my bucket down and starting running! When I got outside of the East Gate, I noticed all of my co-workers standing outside of Lafayette Square Park. I said to myself, nobody told me anything but the Secret Service. Had it not been for the Secret Service, I could have been still there because I never knew the White House was set to be bombed. Although we had looked at it on CSPAN, I had no idea they were headed for the White House. Everybody got orders but me. I started running so fast that the Gingerbread Man couldn't catch me!

President George W. Bush was a two-term President. However, my tenure ended during his first term. It was under this administration that I retired from my position with the White House Staff. While working for this administration, I was standing on a 12-foot ladder washing windows and when I went to step down I missed one of the rungs on the ladder. As I missed the rung and stepped back down on the floor I tore a tendon in my knee. Immediately after I pulled the tendon in my knee, I reported it to my supervisor, Mrs. Limerick. She told me to take off and go to the hospital to check my knee out. The private physician x-rayed my knee and informed me that I had a torn tendon in my knee and would be required to have surgery on my knee. As a result, I took therapy on that particular knee for over a year. After being off so long, I got a call from Mrs. Crans-Limerick regarding my return back to work. I then told her to give me a second to discuss it with my wife. That's when my wife told me, "You said that God had brought you from down there and I don't think you should go back because your job as you once knew it is over. You will never be able to climb ladders and scaffolds again." Then they placed me on

Workmen's Compensation for 2-3 years. The doctor also said that I would not be capable of performing my job as before and after being on Compensation, this was certainly a documented fact. I could no longer perform in my usual capacity. However, he stated that I could work in a lighter profession that did not require bending, stooping, or lifting. The White House offered me the profession of a Secretariat Administrative staff person. I had no professional training for the new job, nor the skillset for administrative work consisting of typing, information technology, and the use of the computer or information technology. The new position would require me to wear a suit each day. It's awesome and extremely amazing how I went from a blue collar worker to a white collar worker without any professional training to prepare me for the job. The doctor told me that I could walk only so many miles a day. The White House staff had removed my privileges to drive in and park each day and had taken away my parking space and sticker that I had been accustomed to utilizing for 34 years. I was then required to ride the Metro, which was much further than I was supposed to walk in order to get to work.

Based on my medical condition and the physicians' report, I was basically forced out of work and did not return back to the White House to accept this position since I did not meet the qualifications of being an administrative assistant and working in an office setting; sitting at a desk was not for me. My position of being the White House Chandelier Polisher had come to an end.

"Greetings everyone, the new President arrives today, President George W. Bush. I wonder what he's like?" wondered one of the White House workers. "He may have a style somewhat like President George H.W. Bush since that is his father." "Yeah, well it will be interesting," someone said. The first year started off rather mild and everyone pretty much had their jobs down. "Hello, Steve. You're one fascinating guy and you seem so low-key." "I am that alright. Why be uptight about anything? I'll pass on that. Anyway, I know who I am and am confident with my techniques and all to perform and keep things in top-notch condition so that when the new Commander in Chief is sworn in, I'm not worried at all," he said. "The atmosphere has changed already," said one of the workers. "Maybe it has, but I do what I know to do to the best of my ability and it's best to remain focused and not change just because everything around you is changing. That's how I've made it so far," said Steve.

A year and some months had gone by. On a brisk September morning, Steve arrived at work at exactly 6:00 am. The morning sun shone through the clouds but somehow the sky had a gloomy overcast. "Attention, Everyone! Please drop whatever you are doing and come to the main conference room; the Twin Towers in New York City are being bombed and the President of the United States is on CSPAN giving a speech to the American people." Everyone rushed in a panic to get to the large conference room. Sobs of everyone permeated the room. When the announcement to drop whatever they were doing happened, Steve never heard it since he was in the lower part of the White House. "Oh my, somebody help me! Where is everybody?" The Secret Service hollered out, "Steve, Steve you better run and all I could think about was getting home to my family." "I need to call my wife," he said." "Oh my, I can't reach her." As he continued to call home he could not reach her due to the phones lines being all tied up.

Shortly thereafter, one day while working, he cried out, "Someone help me! I stepped back off the rung on the ladder." Mrs. Crans-Limerick called out, "Are you okay Steve? I think you had better go get that leg checked out." "I think I'll take you up on that Mrs. Crans- Limerick." He left and went to the hospital and found a treating physician. "Well, Mr. Stevens, it looks as if you have a torn ligament and you will be out of work for a while," said the physician.

Wednesday, February 19, 2016

To Steve: Thanks for the
letter & your good service
at the White House. You
can use the photos, &
I look forward to your
book — Jimmy Carter

"Mrs. Crans-Limerick, I'll have to be out of work for a while and the physician will send over the recommendation for the surgery. I had started enjoying life, spending it with my wife, because the time that I had been working, I had never had that much time with my family.

"Hello, may I speak with Mr. Stewart Stevens please?" "Sure, hold on please. Calvin! The telephone's for you, and it may be someone from work," said Marie. "Ok, honey, I'm coming. Hello, Mrs. Crans-Limerick! Well, I'm recuperating, but things aren't as great as I thought. Thank you so much for calling out of concern." "When do you think you will be returning back to work or are you going to retire?" "Well, I'm not sure," I must discuss this with my wife and I'll get back to you within a day or so."

The next day he returned the call to his supervisor. "Hello, Mrs. Crans-Limerick," said Steve. "Mrs. Crans-Limerick is no longer your supervisor," a man's voice said loud and plain. "Well, thank you very much, but I don't believe I'll be returning to duty because the physician's reports states that I can no longer climb ladders or scaffolds." "Well, we have a solution for you, Steve. You come on back because we have a job for you and you will be able to dress up and wear suits every day to work in the office. But you will also have to catch the Metro and walk about 10 blocks to get here. Your privileges for driving in and parking in the assigned space with a parking pass have been suspended. As a part of the job, you are required to use the computer and schedule meetings for the contractors," the man said. "Oh, that's okay, but I think I'll just go ahead and retire."

This dilemma forced Steve into retirement. He retired and bowed out gracefully to spend the remaining years loving his wife up until the end. He spends all his spare time with family and friends, traveling and telling the story of his life and reminiscing as the White House Chandelier Polisher and window washer.

~ The End ~

IN HONORARIUM OF THE 44TH PRESIDENT, BARACK H. OBAMA

Administration: 2008-2017

Dear Mr. President,

There are books and there are books. However, this is the story of my life at the U.S. White House life. In my opinion, you have performed in the most superior manner as the first African American President of the United States of America. While working for seven Presidents, my only regret is that I was not afforded the opportunity to work for you. I have much respect and admiration for you as the first African American Presidential trail blazer. You and the First Lady and your family will go down in history – our history. Your First Lady, Michelle Obama, has been a very supportive, strong, youthful and endearing woman. In 2012, while out to dinner with my wife, I mentioned how much I would like the opportunity to have worked under your administration and to have personally met you and your wife. When I watched your inauguration ceremony, I felt very proud, with a true sense of belonging as an American citizen. This has all moved me emotionally since my wife and I have been married for 55 years. Everything you said you would do when taking the oath of office you tried with all your power to do. Your unrelenting spirit and your ability to stick with what you believed is admirable. You never gave up in the face of adversity, even with the challenges that the nation faced. During my time of working at the White House, I would often see the other Presidents coming down the White House corridors and going to the Oval Office. They would stop and speak and greet me by name, and we got on friendly basis that I enjoyed very much. I know you and I would have shared similar experiences had I been working at the White House under your Presidency. I have noticed that you and the First Lady have high family values and you have a close relationship with each other that bears a strong resemblance to the relationship of my wife and I. I especially like a lot of your slogans, such as "Yes We Can" and "Yes We Did." I like your laid-back swag because I used to swag myself when I was younger man. We hope that you, your wife, and your family enjoy your stay in Washington DC after completion of your Presidential administration and I wish you the best!

TRIBUTE TO THE FIRST LADIES

To All of the First Ladies:

You are wonderfully and specially designed to carry on the mission of standing beside and supporting your husbands while they serve as the President of the United States of America.

As the First Ladies, you share the brunt of what concerns your husband during times of crisis when serving as the President of the United States of America. Whatever affected them had an effect on you as well.

It was a true pleasure and honor to work for you all, to support you and your family during your tenure in the White House. Quite honestly, the Presidents would not have had the opportunity of serving this country as effectively and efficiently had it not been for you, the First Ladies.

I would like to offer my condolences to the Reagan family on the loss of a very dear First Lady and wife of President Ronald W. Reagan, Mrs. Nancy Reagan. I recall working for First Lady Mrs. Reagan while working in the White House as the Chandelier Polisher and window washer. It is an emotional time for me with the loss of Mrs. Reagan because I am writing a book of my life story about working at the White House and I sure wish that she would have had the opportunity of reading my book before passing. I recall when Mrs. Reagan gave me a few gifts. One of the souvenirs is a Red ballpoint ink pen with her name signed on it. She loved Red; Red was her favorite color. She gave me a Red and Gold bookmark and one of her favorite portraits of her dressed in Red evening gown.

A photo First lady nancy Reagan; A Red autographed pen from Nancy Reagan.

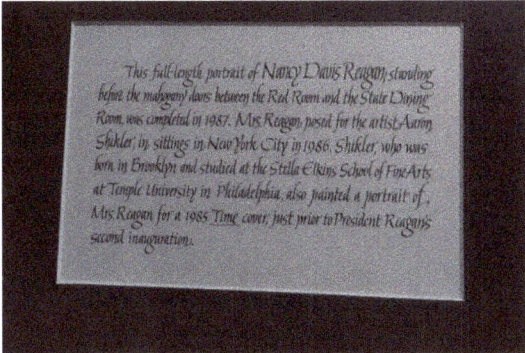

This full-length portrait of Nancy Davis Reagan, standing before the mahogany doors between the Red Room and the State Dining Room, was completed in 1987. Mrs. Reagan posed for the artist Aaron Shikler, in sittings in New York City in 1986. Shikler, who was born in Brooklyn and studied at the Stella Elkins School of Fine Arts at Temple University in Philadelphia, also painted a portrait of Mrs. Reagan for a 1985 Time cover, just prior to President Reagan's second inauguration.

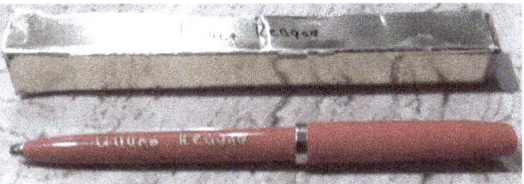

(Courtesy of Stewart C. Stevens Sr.)

And I know without my love, my only love, it would have been impossible to perform my job because she was truly my First Lady. She kept me going when I was stressed out about the amount of work and hours I was doing at the White House. When I was working, my wife was always there to encourage me. She assured me that everything would work out – and it did!

I Thank God for All the First Ladies

ADVICE TO THE YOUNG GENERATION

Stewart was always giving advice to young men. When he told his story out in public, there were groups of young men that asked him questions of how he was able to do what he did. "Mr. Stevens, were you afraid of height? "Uh…Mr. Stevens you went away to the National Guard at such a young age…what made you do that…didn't you want to just be a normal teen?" Mr. Stevens you had such an underprivileged childhood, didn't that make you want to get into something to let out some of that negative energy?" Stewart always gave a positive response to the youth. He gave the advice of a mentor encouraging them to keep out of trouble and try to connect with positive people, "Stay away from trouble!" Lynetta recalls, Stewart spoke at an historical event at the Benjamin Banneker Museum, MD.

(Courtesy of Lynetta Stevens)

After the event, he connected with a youth group and responded to their questions. The young men's mother brought them there to simply learn something from Stewart Stevens Sr. They were really impressed and so was he! Stewart was impressed at how tuned into his advice; they were like soaking it all in! As a result of the effects on these guys, Stewart had plans for using his story to become a motivational speaker, pre-pandemic. After the pandemic, everything unfortunately changed. Life happens

Stewart "Calvin" was a wonderful great-grandfather. His little great-grandson tagged along with us during the book events and speaking engagements for the past 10 years. How unique and rewarding was that! He was kind of like a drill sergeant even at home sometime. Stewart liked when you said, "Yes Sir" as a form of respect.

*As a younger uncle, "**Uncle Calvin**" as his nephews recall, gave instructions on life and shared small talk. He had an encouraging word here and there for his sons, nephews, and grandchildren ....for the boys and girls. He took time out of his daily routine and during visits to speak about life from his perspective; joke around and play humorously with them!*

(Courtesy of Stewart C. Stevens Sr.)

THIS IS WHAT I would like to tell the younger generation. When working in any profession, I would gently advise you to do the following. These are my words of wisdom:

- Ensure that you have good education so that when o**pportunity meets Destiny simultaneously: You Will Be Ready!** Meaning, when the opportunity arises you can walk right into that door. If you choose a trade rather than college education, master it well so you will be the best at what you do!

- Ensure that you keep a **clean record, reputation, and credibility.** Stay away from conversations that lead to gossip, which will lead to trouble.

- Ensure you are familiar with and value **office ethics and policies; stay away from discussing politics and religion at work.**

- **Do your work with diligence!** If you have downtime, find time to observe others and learn something new. Be willing to be flexible and assist with projects beyond what you were hired to do. **By stepping in and helping others, you will remain a valuable asset to your agency or organization.**

- **Practice being courteous and kind, but do not intermingle personal life with work life.** You never know with whom you are sharing personal family secrets and that person could someday become your manager or vice versa. It is a small world!

- **Protect your family and personal life and do not share; protect your image.** It will be a bad reflection on you to divulge personal details of your family. Keep the job out of your family circle and likewise be confidential concerning work matters, especially if you have sworn to an oath of office.

- Practice **integrity, honesty, and truth.**

- Ensure that you treat everyone with respect and do not slander. If someone comes to you with a piece of garbage, do not get involved and take that on. **Listen, but be slow to offer any comments or opinions.**

- When interviewing and even after you are hired for a position, **Dress your Way to success!** Young men, keep a belt around your pants and pull them up, tidy and neat. Young women protect your modesty. **Don't sell yourself cheap and remain discreet. Respect yourself and others will too!**

HISTORICAL NOTES

The picture of George Washington:

When Dolly Madison heard that the British were on the way to burn the White House down, she had taken the picture of George Washington, the first President, off the wall and saved it. It hangs in the East Room today. George Washington was the only President that never lived in the White House. The British burning it in 1814 did not completely destroy the White House because of a good hard rain.

North Portico and South Portico of the White House:

The White House is the only house that does not have a front door and a back door. Rather, it has a North Portico and a South Portico. The North Portico is for Kings and Queens to enter. The South Portico is for White House staff and those other than Kings and Queens to enter.

The original Wood of the White House:

The original inside of the White House was made out of special wood. All of the wood did not burn in when the British set it afire in 1814. I was given two ashtrays made out of part of the White House original wood after the British had left. The ashtrays have a brass tag on them stating, "This is part of the original White House wood." This is a picture of the ashtray souvenirs made from original White House wood. They were given to me by the White House carpenters who carved them.

(Courtesy of Stewart C. Stevens Sr.)

The White House Easter Egg Roll:

The White House Easter Egg Roll was held on the south grounds of the White House. The history of the White House Easter Egg Roll, which begins at one end of Pennsylvania Avenue and continues at the other, is one of the oldest and most unique traditions in presidential history. Rolling eggs on the Monday after Easter was a tradition observed by many Washington families, including those of the President. Some historians believe Dolly Madison first suggested the idea of a public egg roll, while others tell stories of informal egg- rolling parties at the White House dating back to President Lincoln's day. Public egg-rolling celebrations, however, were held not at the White House, but on the grounds of the Capitol. During my time at the White House it was held on the South grounds of the White House.

During one of the Easter Egg Rolls at the White House, celebrities were guests at the Easter Egg Roll. I have one Easter egg personally autographed by President Reagan. I was very fortunate to get all of their signatures on the Easter Eggs. All of the Presidents presented me with Easter eggs; many famous people personally autographed the eggs and handed them to me. I have them all in my personal collection of souvenirs.

(Courtesy of Stewart C. Stevens Sr.)

The Windows of the White House:

The original windows were not destroyed thanks to the rain that stopped the burning of the White House in 1814. In 1952 the White House was renovated, but the windows did not have UV Protection and without UV protection, furnishings were not protected and the wall interior became damaged from the sun. Two other employees and me worked together to install the clear 3M film over the windows. Once the film was adequately installed, the windows looked as they did initially. One thing I really regret is that I never had an actual accounting of the number of windows, chandeliers, or light globes. I was only hired to clean them all, not to count them all! This shows that I was doing my job – just cleaning and polishing, not counting.

BEHIND THE SCENES GALLERY OF THE WHITEHOUSE PORTRAITS

THE WATER PAINTING OF the Green Room Presented to Stewart C. Stevens by President Bill Clinton and First Lady

(Courtesy of Stewart C. Stevens Sr.)

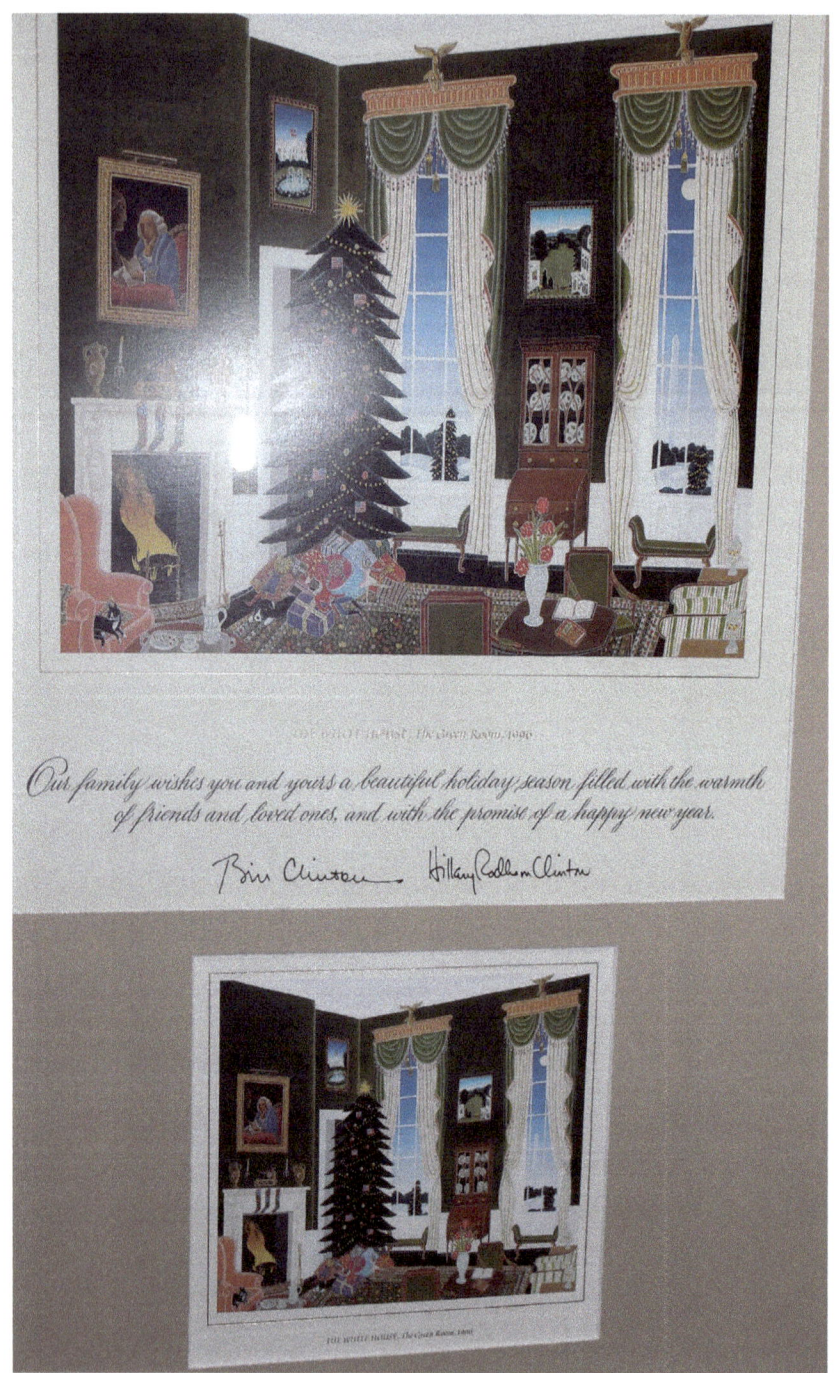

THE WHITE HOUSE, The Green Room, 1999

Our family wishes you and yours a beautiful holiday season filled with the warmth of friends and loved ones, and with the promise of a happy new year.

Bill Clinton   Hillary Rodham Clinton

THE WHITE HOUSE, The Green Room, 1999

STEWART CALVIN STEVENS SR.

STEWART C. STEVENS WAS born in Washington, DC and raised as a native Washingtonian. He came from very humble beginnings. Stewart was educated in the Washington, DC public school system and attended Browne Jr. High school, which was named in honor of Hugh Mason Browne, a Black American pioneer. Hugh Mason Browne was an influential educator and creative thinker whose ideas were a part of the early development of African American education and civil rights. Although Stewart did not have much education, he had more than earned a degree in the University of Adversity during the course of his life.

Stewart went on to a career with the National Guard Army which took him abroad to various military bases in the United States, Heidelberg Germany, and back home to his family and friends. Although he trained as a Military Police officer, he faced various challenges in the 1950s thanks to discrimination and never became the policeman he dreamt of becoming.

Later, Stewart developed a talent for cleaning and washing windows but he was gifted with Chandelier polishing. This skillset was developed before working for the White House with an established small business while working with a brother in the early 1960s. Stewart went on to marry Janice M. Bryant and start a family.

As Stewart shares his life story before and after the White House and all his experiences. He also shares some historical events, views of society, and advice to others as it relates to how he performed his job and how he faced challenges while working for seven Presidents over the course of 34 years.

Stewart shares the White House with readers through portraits, photos, memorabilia, souvenirs autographed by Presidents, Diplomats and celebrities, along with personal and intimate photos of himself and his family.

Stewart Calvin Stevens is a man of rare essence!

(Courtesy of White House Photographer)

(Courtesy of White House Photographer)

PRESIDENTIAL REMARKS ABOUT STEWART C. STEVENS SR

Dear Stewart,

I do want you to know that I am mindful and deeply appreciative of your cooperation and your commitment, and for the tolerance shown by your family and friends at the over-long hours you put in—not just for me, but for the big job we are all trying to do together.

-President Gerald R. Ford, 38th President

Dear Stewart,

In the performance of your duties you have always shown your multiple awareness of these multiple meanings at the White house, you've helped keep it a hearth of warmth for Nancy and me and a house of welcome for visitors and dignitaries from every part of this nation and the world.

-President, Ronald W. Reagan, 40th President

Dear Mr. Stevens,

Thank you for your personal efforts toward the success of our state visits honoring their majesties the Emperor and Express of Japan, President and Mrs. Yeltsin and President Mandela. The President and I deeply appreciate your dedication and teamwork and look forward to working with you to welcome other heads of state to the White house.

-Hillary Rodham Clinton, First lady, 42nd President Clinton

(Courtesy of Lynetta Stevens)

(Courtesy of Lynetta Stevens)

www.ingramcontent.com/pod-product-compliance
Lightning Source LLC
Chambersburg PA
CBHW051155120626
46547CB00012B/1074